Guidebook

— FOR —

CONFESSORS

Guidebook
— FOR —
CONFESSORS

REV. MICHAEL E. GIESLER

Scepter

Nihil Obstat: Donald F. Haggerty, S.T.D., *Censor Librorum*
Imprimatur: + Timothy M. Dolan, D.D., Archbishop of New York

Copyright © 2010, Scepter Publishers, Inc.
P.O. Box 211, New York, N.Y. 10018
www.scepterpublishers.org

Text design: Carol Sawyer/Rose Design

Printed in the United States of America

ISBN-13: 978-1-59417-091-1

This book is dedicated to all priests, ministers
of Christ's mercy and forgiveness, and in a special way
to Saints John Marie Vianney and Josemaría Escrivá—
both of whom served so many souls through their
dedication and love for the Sacrament of Penance.

Contents

SECTION VI

SECTION VII

SECTION VIII

SECTION IX

APPENDICES

Foreword

Confession, at times, appears to be the forgotten sacrament. It is too often neglected or shunned as the normal means of being reconciled to God and the Church, of growing in grace, and persevering in authentic holiness of life. And if it is avoided by the faithful, then it is fair to say that we, as priests and priest confessors, have not always placed it as high on our list of pastoral priorities as it deserves.

In this Year for Priests, and invoking the prayerful assistance of St. John Marie Vianney, patron of pastors, Fr. Michael Giesler gives us this *Guidebook for Confessors*. It is a brief but well-packed compendium that can help us renew our love of the Sacrament of Reconciliation. It offers a clear summary of the theology of sin, forgiveness, and grace. It is a primer on the Rite of the Sacrament, and a practical "how to" reference book for helping people make an integral and fruitful confession.

Fr. Giesler is both a worthy theologian and an experienced practitioner whose love for priests, penitents, and the sacrament shines through each page. Here he helps us discover the priest as a minister of God's mercy. Though the *Guidebook* may be helpful to seminary professors and newer priests, it offers insights and reminders for more seasoned confessors as well. I found many helpful reflections here, and a good outline of the questions and challenges the confessor faces, with some strategies and recommendations. I was most enthusiastic to see such a good handbook offered in a manner that was encouraging to both priests and penitents.

Acting in the person of Christ and as the representative of the Church, the priest in the confessional has the joy of announcing God's pardon and peace. I know that many will find in the *Guidebook for Confessors* an impetus and aid for renewing our love of and commitment to this sacrament of God's mercy.

MOST REVEREND ROBERT W. FINN
Bishop of Kansas City-St. Joseph

Section I

The Universal Call to Holiness

Through their baptismal vocation all the faithful receive within them the seed of divine life, sanctifying grace, which should increase throughout their lives. Each man and woman is called to become another Christ, *alter Christus*, with a deep and personal life of prayer and a true commitment to the good of their neighbor. This is a demanding vocation, and many times they will fail because of the effects of original sin, and their own personal weaknesses. For this reason there is need for a sacrament that will not only forgive sins, but give the faithful grace to overcome their faults, and to provide them sustenance in their journey towards God.

The Sacrament of Confession has the unique power of uprooting and cleansing the principle obstacles to our sanctity . . . those thoughts, words, actions, and omissions that take us from God, and leave a residue of guilt and punishment in our souls. At the same time Reconciliation gives us a grace and peace of mind that brings us closer to Christ himself, as Mary Magadalene, Zacchaeus, and Peter did when they humbly admitted their sins. In other words, the Sacrament of Confession truly helps us all—priests and lay faithful—to fulfill Christ's universal command to his followers, **"Be holy as your heavenly father is holy"** (Mt 5:48).

The Sacrament of Confession is also the sacrament of conversion, a point stressed frequently by Saint Josemaría Escrivá both in his preaching and writings: "Human life is in some way a constant returning to our Father's house. We return through contrition, through the conversion of heart, which means a desire to change, a firm decision to improve our life and which, therefore, is expressed in sacrifice and self-giving. We return to our Father's house by means of that sacrament of pardon in which, by confessing our sins, we put on Jesus Christ again and become his brothers, members of God's family" (*Christ Is Passing By*, 64. Scepter Publishers, New York, NY).

Using the parable of the prodigal son as inspiration, he further states that penance is a sacrament of joy: "God is waiting for us, like the father in the parable, with open arms, even though we don't deserve it. It doesn't matter how great our debt is. Just like the prodigal son, all we have to do is open our heart, to be homesick for our Father's house, to wonder and rejoice in the gift which God makes us of being able to call ourselves his children, of really being his children, even though our response to him has been so poor" (*Christ Is Passing By*, 64. Scepter Publishers, New York, NY).

Reconciliation has repercussions upon the entire people of God as well. The more it is received, the more holy families become, with positive effects for entire communities and nations. It enables people to be less egotistical, and more thoughtful of those around them. It helps them to examine their motives and failings frequently, not only as private persons, but as family members, colleagues, and fellow citizens. For this reason we can affirm that every good confession not only helps the individual man or woman to become more holy, but enables the entire Church to become more holy . . . since through the contrition and penance of her members she draws closer to her Bridegroom. We could even say that all mankind is helped by good confessions, since God's grace and forgiveness will extend through those who have been forgiven to those still far away from God.

Jesus Christ Forgives Throughout the Centuries

No sacrament can be understood outside of its living context, which is the Mystical Body of Christ. The Sacrament of Confession is part of Christ's perennial love and service to his faithful throughout the centuries. It is the result of his Incarnation and his salvific mission to the human race.

Like all the sacraments, Penance is intrinsically connected with the liturgy, since it is a form of praise to God by his Church: indeed all of the sacraments are celebrations that draw the faithful closer to God. Baptized into the death and resurrection of Christ, they are members of his Body on earth. Priests have the mission of serving all the faithful through these sacraments. In the words of the *Catholic Catechism, the ordained priesthood guarantees that it really is Christ who acts in the sacraments through the Holy Spirit for the Church* (*Catechism of the Catholic Church* [*CCC*], 1120).

Therefore it is not the individual priest who forgives sins; it is **Christ working through him**. For this reason the Church has taught that the sacraments work *ex opere operato*, by virtue of the saving work of Christ, accomplished once for all. In other words, by the very act of the sacrament being performed—with a valid minister, and the prescribed matter and form—absolution and grace are conferred.

Within the classification of the sacraments, both Penance and Anointing are called sacraments of healing. Through them the sinner is reconciled with God, the Church, and truly, with himself. If he was in the state of mortal sin, his sin is forgiven in God's eyes, he is restored to union with the Church, and he is strengthened in his personal life to be more faithful to God. Pope John Paul in his apostolic exhortation on Penance summarized these points in terms of reconciliation: *The forgiven penitent is reconciled with himself in his inmost being, where he regains his innermost truth. He is reconciled with his brethren whom he has in some way offended and wounded. He is reconciled with the Church. He is reconciled with all creation.* (John Paul II, *Apostolic Exhortation on Reconciliation and Penance*, Dec. 2, 1984, no. 31, 5). If the sinner has made a good and sincere confession, he will experience in some way the joy and wholeness that the prodigal son experienced when his father forgave him, and welcomed him back to his home (cf. Lk 15:11–24).

The foundation and existence of the Sacrament of Penance presupposes—of course—the fact of sin in the human race, both original and personal. We do not have a perfect nature; because of the sin of Adam and Eve our nature is flawed and has evil tendencies, one of which is concupiscence. The Church rejected Martin Luther's teaching that human nature is totally corrupted by sin, yet she has always held that our nature is fallen and is in constant need of healing and forgiveness.

The confession of sins to an ordained minister of Christ is part of the mystery of Redemption. Through this sacrament Christ the High Priest, and only Victim for sins, applies the merit of his Passion, death, and resurrection to the sinner. Indeed all the sacraments derive their power from Christ's paschal mystery. In the Sacrament of Penance, the merit which Jesus earned on the cross through his obedience is applied to the sinner who humbly confesses his disobedience to God. As Pope John Paul II stated in his first encyclical, "*The redemption of the world—this tremendous mystery of love in which creation is renewed—is at its deepest root, the fullness of justice in a human heart—the heart of the first-born Son—in order that it may become justice in the hearts of many human beings . . .* " (Pope John Paul II, *Redemptor Hominis*, March 4, 1979, no. 9).

Sacramental Grace

Besides forgiveness, grace is imparted in every good confession. If the soul is in grave sin, he receives sanctifying grace which had been lost through sin, and the eternal punishment due to his sin is taken away. This allows him once again to share in God's own life—to receive the privilege of the Divine Indwelling within his soul. He is no longer an enemy of God but a friend of God, and even more, he once again forms part of his Divine Family. If the person has confessed venial sins, those sins are forgiven, along with some or all of the temporal punishment due to them, depending on the person's dispositions. His soul increases in sanctifying grace, and he receives a special sacramental grace to avoid those sins in the future.

A good confession is a new opportunity for a person. With God's grace and favor within, he can grow both in human virtue and the supernatural virtues infused into his soul at Baptism. He can live a more perfect life as a son of God, avoid more easily the occasion of sin in the future, and become more and more like Christ. For all of these reasons the Church recommends frequent confession, which *helps us form our conscience, fight against evil tendencies, let ourselves be healed by Christ, and progress in the life of the Spirit (CCC* 1458).

As said above, every sin hurts the community of God's people on earth—but every good confession heals and restores that people once again. It is the Church herself, having obtained her power through Christ the Savior, who intercedes for the sinner, and desires him to be reintegrated into her community. This is actually affirmed in the words said immediately before absolution: **"Through the ministry of the Church may God give you pardon and peace. . . . "** No sin therefore is totally personal or individual.

Throughout his life and especially on the cross Christ atoned for sins: he literally put "at one" the alienated human race with his Father God. He confided the grace of that atonement to his Church, who like a good Mother applies it to us in the sacrament of pardon. As such his atonement is infinite because he is an infinite Person. But we too must do our part to show sorrow for sins and make atonement or satisfaction for them. This is the meaning of the penance that we voluntarily accept and carry out as part of the sacrament. It is what the Church desires us to do in order to show our union with the atoning Christ, who makes up for all sins through his sacrifice.

It is also a consequence of our recognition that we are responsible for our lives and actions. If we were not free, if we had no option but to choose sin, why should we make atonement for it? There would be no need to do so.

Some Helpful Preliminaries
for the Priest Confessor

Classical Insights into Human Nature
and the Moral Law

Besides knowing the theology and effects of sacramental confession, we priests should know a bit of psychology, first of all the rational psychology of the great classical philosophers, which distinguishes the various faculties of the human soul, namely intellect, free will, memory, imagination, and emotions. Most likely we studied some of these ideas in the seminary, but it might be worthwhile for us to review these basic truths now and again. Knowing how human beings are "put together" is necessary for making good judgments in confession about the state of a person's soul, that is, how responsible he is for his actions, and what advice to give him. Sound philosophy and reasoning tell us that the highest faculties of the soul are the intellect and free will, which properly characterize the human person, who is made in the image and likeness of God (cf. Gen 1:27). Human beings have the capacity to know the natural or moral law within them, which is really a participation in the eternal law of God, and which shows them the way to true happiness. Its most basic message is *to do good and avoid evil*, from which flow certain moral principles that are well summarized in the Ten Commandments. Many times this knowledge is clouded over by sin, or bad habits, but it can never be completely removed from a person's soul.

There may be cases when a person has what is called invincible ignorance, that is, he or she is not culpable for ignoring certain moral truths because of their environment, upbringing, or the confused advice that they have been given. But every human being has the obligation to form his conscience well, so that he can make true and certain judgments about what is right or wrong. Part of our work in the confessional is precisely to help people to form their consciences properly.

If moral truth exists as a kind of light in the intellect, moral goodness exists as an attraction of the will. Man by nature wants what is good and that which will lead him to his ultimate fulfillment and happiness. But his will is also free and capable of making wrong decisions, which lead him away from that fulfillment and happiness. The will is often disturbed by strong emotions or passions such as fear, anger, or lust, and therefore needs to be strengthened or perfected by a life of virtue. Such passions can diminish, and on rare occasion, even take away responsibility for a particular action. Virtue is obtained by the repetition of good actions, while vice originates by the repetition of bad actions.

We shouldn't consider the above truths to be only theoretical, but they are grounded in common sense and the objective experience of human actions and motivations. With knowledge of these basic facts about moral truth and people's dispositions, we can understand a penitent's struggles more easily and objectively, and will be able to give the best advice to him or her.

Mental and Emotional Disorders

At the same time we should know a bit about the major mental and emotional disorders that people can suffer, and how they can affect a person's judgments and free will. Perhaps we ourselves have suffered from such disorders, to a greater or lesser degree. Clinical depression, bipolar disease, obsessive compulsiveness, and anxiety disorders can have a strong influence on the way people see themselves and others, and in many cases can disturb their judgment on what is right or wrong. These diseases also affect a person's free will, so that he cannot choose an action with complete freedom. If a person in confession tells us of his condition beforehand, we can make a much better judgment and give appropriate advice and encouragement to him, while not making false excuses for him. At other times we may simply be able to tell that there is something abnormal in the person's speech or reasoning, and in those moments we will have to ask the Holy Spirit for the grace to respond appropriately—not completely ruling out the possibility of sin for such an individual, but encouraging and guiding him in a compassionate way.

Addictive behavior, such as to alcohol or pornography, must also be considered for what it is: though *materially* (that is, as far as the action itself) a penitent may be committing grave sins, *formally* (that is, as far as his personal responsibility) he may not be guilty of mortal sin since his ability to reject the temptation is sorely weakened, and he is much less free. We should take this into account, lest we judge the person too severely. For such behaviors, we could have some good references to give to the person, preferably outside of confession, for professional treatment—since often this will be required for overcoming the addiction, or at least lessening it. A related field is the influence of drugs on a person's mind and decision-making capacity. In all these cases, it would appear that moral responsibility is most serious at the beginning of acquiring the addiction, when the person had sufficient awareness and freedom to choose or reject the disordered action, but instead decided to give in to it. In the case of an addict, this initial decision to commit grave sin is what needs to be confessed, though he should also confess his present addictive actions for any degree of willfulness or consent that they have, and be willing to amend his life as best as he can, despite his weakened state.

Some penitents react well and can rid themselves of addiction to pornography and other sins of the flesh if they remember Jesus' words: **"Let your yes be yes, and your no, no! What is outside of that is from the evil one"** (Mt 5:37). Addiction causes one to be ambivalent: *Yes*, the person seems to say, *I want to get rid of this, but no, I can't.* . . . Therefore, his or her "no" has to be an emphatic **No**. One priest friend of mine gives the example of a lion tamer who faces a lion (which can be compared to sensuality)—with a chair in one hand (which can be compared to prayer and penance), and a whip in the other. He doesn't crack the whip to hurt the lion but to scare the lion. The lion is more frightened by fear than by actual pain. In the same way a person can scare away his sensuality, to a certain extent. If he is tempted, he must vigorously cry out **"No!"**

Differences between Men and Women

It is also most helpful for us, as priest confessors, to be aware of the differences between male and female psychology. While the moral law is obviously the same for both men and women, the good priest confessor will be able to say things in different ways for different persons. Often times it is more effective with women to use a lighter and gentler tone of voice, stressing the idea of love and relationship with God and others. With men we can be more direct and forceful, emphasizing the challenge to become a saint and the need to struggle in certain areas. In a more specific way these differences apply to married couples, since the happiness of the one is intimately bound to the happiness of the other. At times we may have to enlighten the man about the woman's emotional need to be understood and cherished, while we may need to enlighten the woman about the man's need for more physical intimacy. In delicate but clear terms we should also be able to explain in few words the beauty and dignity of the conjugal act, and how contraceptive behavior violates the nature of the act, the intimate nature of a man and a woman, and the self-giving of the couple to one another. The writings of Pope John Paul II could be most helpful in this regard, especially his thoughts on the *Theology of the Body*, and the complementary nature of male and female sexuality. At given times we can recommend the practice known as natural family planning (NFP), if there is a serious reason to avoid a pregnancy, or if the couple wishes to conceive a child and therefore must know the woman's cycles and fertility better.

Children and their Development

In the case of children, at least beginning with the age of reason, we must understand and guide them according to their age and grasp of the moral law. Between the ages of seven to twelve, boys and girls have a clear and simple view of what is right and wrong; they are particularly sensitive to, and also prone to, lacks of justice and charity in dealing with others, as well as to telling lies or disobedience to their parents. They are more open to the need for prayer, and implicitly understand its value. It is good to give them simple things to do and to think about. When puberty arrives however (usually earlier for girls than for boys), there are more complicated issues at stake, especially peer pressure, self-esteem, desire for independence, and sexuality. These are years when the priest confessor must be particularly patient and encouraging, while aware of the changes that these young people are experiencing in their lives. In an encouraging and helpful way we can keep them struggling to be good disciples of Christ, without watering down the moral law or its demands.

Finally, whenever we hear confessions, it is good to end on a positive note. Whether the person has committed grave sins or lighter ones, he or she should always emerge from the confessional enlightened and encouraged. Many times it is helpful to give them some small, but realistic goal that they can accomplish. In this way they know that we have confidence in them, and that we are praying for them. They will understand that they have not only been forgiven in their confession, but in a special way they have also been *loved*.

In this text, *CCC* refers to the abbreviation for the *Catechism of the Catholic Church* (1994) and *CIC* to the *Code of Canon Law* (1993).

Section II

A Brief History of the Sacrament

As said above, Jesus Christ, Savior of every human being, works in a personal and powerful way through the Sacrament of Penance, as he does in all the sacraments. Though as God he is free to forgive men in his own way, he has established the Sacrament of Penance as the ordinary way that he does this on earth—through his Church and his ordained ministers, who impart absolution in his name and by his divine power.

The institution of Penance took place after the Resurrection, when Christ appeared to the apostles, and after breathing upon them, said: **"Receive the Holy Spirit. If you forgive the sins of any, they are forgiven; if you retain the sins of any, they are retained"** (Jn 20:22–23). Before this, he had promised the power to forgive sins to Peter as head of the Church: **"I will give you the keys of the kingdom of heaven, and whatever you bind on earth shall be bound in heaven, and whatever you loose on earth shall be loosed in heaven"** (Mt 16:19). Quoting from Vatican II's *Lumen Gentium*, the *Catechism* states that *"the office of binding and loosing which was given to Peter was also assigned to the college of the apostles united to the head"* (*CCC* 1444).

The various names for the sacrament used throughout the centuries give some idea of its nature and purpose. It is called the Sacrament of *Conversion* since the follower of Christ desires to make a clear step towards coming back to God, and to receive his grace. It is called the Sacrament of *Penance*, since the sinner is willing to make up for his offenses by doing an act of satisfaction or penance, in order to manifest his sorrow in a specific way. It is most frequently called the Sacrament of *Confession*, since the penitent openly and honestly discloses his sins to the priest, entrusting himself to the mercy of God. It is also called the Sacrament of *Forgiveness*, since God takes away the guilt of all who confess their sins with the proper disposition of soul. Finally, a more recent term for the sacrament, coined after the Second Vatican Council, is that of *Reconciliation*, since through his sincere confession the penitent is reconciled or reunited with the Church and with God . . . after sin had separated him.

The Need for Conversion and Purification

Though Baptism takes away original sin and mitigates its effects, it does not take away the tendency to sin. Every baptized person needs forgiveness and renewal if he or she should fall into sin . . . whether of pride, laziness, sensuality, or any other kind of evil. If a person is honest, he will recognize these tendencies within himself, and the voluntary or semi-voluntary thoughts, words, actions, or omissions that come from them: he therefore will have the desire to confess his sins honestly and receive God's forgiveness, and, of course, the grace to do better. Saint John the Apostle put this situation very plainly when he wrote: **"If we say we have no sin, we deceive ourselves, and the truth is not in us"** (1 Jn 1:8). What is more, if a man really desires to become a saint, he will see the need to keep beginning again in his spiritual and personal struggle, receiving the help of Jesus Christ and his ministers in the Church. This continuous conversion after Baptism is not simply a human work. *"It is truly an interior repentance; it is the movement of a 'contrite heart' drawn and moved by grace to respond to the merciful love of God who loved us first"* (CCC 1428).

There are many trends in the modern world which blur the awareness of sin in people's lives. One is the theory that people are not responsible for their actions, and that any bad actions they perform are only the result of their environment or body chemistry. Related to this is the widespread tendency to "psychologize" everything, supplying mental or emotional excuses for the most aberrant behaviors. Another error is to consider sin to be only a medieval concept or prejudice, which has now been superceded by the "liberty" and "progress" of modern man, who is not bound by outmoded commandments or rules. Certain kinds of sin, especially against life and human sexuality, are even held to be modern forms of personal liberation, and are thus justified by many in the media and entertainment industry. Since the existence of the devil and Hell has also been made to appear archaic or ridiculous, people no longer fear God's punishment for their sins. Or if they at least have the honesty to recognize their faults, they are convinced that God's mercy will always forgive them, even if they don't change things.

In addition to the above factors, there has been a greater tendency in the last forty years for many preachers and writers to concentrate on social issues and the responsibilities of Catholics in this area, rather than other demands of God's law, such as the obligation to worship on Sundays, the importance of prayer and atonement, and certain moral obligations relating to the sixth commandment.

As a result fewer Catholics today feel the need to go to confession, or have convinced themselves that sin and forgiveness is really a private matter between them and God. Some have even accepted the idea that confession was a man-made invention (the error of Martin Luther), and not really instituted by Jesus Christ himself. Many Catholics go up to receive Communion regularly every week, but neglect going to confession for a very long time. Without wanting to judge their consciences, one might legitimately ask why they don't see the need for receiving the sacrament of forgiveness more often.

For all the above reasons, we can truly speak of a "crisis" facing the Sacrament of Confession today. There are some signs that it may be mitigating, but past attitudes and habits remain hardened within the minds of many Catholic men and women. We as priests need to be aware of this, and as much as possible we must try to give both instruction and exhortation to our people on how to examine their consciences well—without false excuses or escapisms—and how to confess their sins frequently with true sorrow and purpose of amendment.

To take good advantage of confession, therefore, one must have the humility to think that he really **needs** God's forgiveness and grace. He has to have an awareness of sin . . . his own personal sins, not only the sins of terrorists, rapists, or the monsters of history. If he does not have this awareness, he can easily reject the need for confession, and he runs the grave risk of rejecting Christ himself, who said that he had come **not to call the righteous, but sinners** (Mt 9:13), and whose first words in his ministry were a warning: **"The time is fulfilled, and the kingdom of God is at hand; repent, and believe in the gospel"** (Mk 1:15).

Matter and Form of the Sacrament

Though the terms **matter** and **form** come from a previous theology, they do provide a valid insight into the working of the sacraments and are still helpful to consider, as long as one avoids a certain mechanistic view of them. One could say that the remote matter for the Sacrament of Penance are those sins committed after Baptism. The proximate matter of this sacrament is really the acts of the penitent, which include examination of conscience, contrition for sins committed, and the act of confessing them to the priest or bishop. Just as water is necessary matter for the Sacrament of Baptism, these acts of the penitent are necessary for the validity of the sacrament. If a person does not have contrition for his sins (at least for fear of punishment), if he does not have at least the implicit desire of amendment, or if he does not manifest his sins outwardly to the priest, he cannot receive the sacrament of forgiveness.

The complete form of the sacrament are the words that the minister says after hearing the confession of the penitent. According to the *Ordo Paenitentiae* (no. 19) these are: *"God, the Father of Mercies, through the death and resurrection of his Son, has reconciled the world* to himself and sent the Holy Spirit among us for the forgiveness of sins. Through the ministry of the Church, may God give you pardon and peace. **And I absolve you from your sins in the name + of the Father, and of the Son, and of the Holy Spirit**.

May the Passion of our Lord Jesus Christ, the intercession of the Blessed Virgin Mary and of all the saints, whatever good you do, and suffering you endure, heal your sins, help you to grow in holiness, and reward you with eternal life. Go in peace."

OR: *"The Lord has freed you from your sins. Go in peace."*

Within this form, the essential words of absolution are **"I absolve you from your sins, in the name of the Father, and of the Son, and of the Holy Spirit."** In urgent cases, such as danger of death, only these words can be used without employing the full formula stated above. Also the last part of the formula that begins *May the Passion . . .* can be omitted in particular cases, in case of need, such as the presence of a very large number of penitents waiting for confession. The absolution should be spoken and the penitent needs to be close enough to be able to hear them; absolution by phone or electronic devices is not valid. We should say the words of absolution clearly and with expression—not mumble or garble them, or say them in a routine or bored tone of voice. Apart from their spiritual effect, the words as the form of the sacrament are beautiful, and in themselves they can bring great peace and confidence to the person hearing them.

After many confessions, our voices may become strained, but we can always make the effort to say the words properly, even in a lower voice. On rare occasion: the priest may have to give a conditional absolution, for instance if a person is in danger of death at the scene of an accident, or in a hospital. In these cases he may not know if the person is truly sorry for his or her sins, or is even a Catholic, but the person's salvation could be at stake if absolution is not given. Such absolution can be preceded with the words *si capax es* "if you are capable"—that is, if you have the right dispositions, or if you are still alive, I absolve you from your sins.

Celebrating the Sacrament of Penance

Quoting from the *Ordo Paenitentiae* of the Second Vatican Council, the *Catechism* states that *"individual, integral confession and absolution remain the only ordinary way for the faithful to reconcile themselves with God and the Church, unless physical or moral impossibility excuses from this kind of confession"* (CCC 1484). This practice, going back to the earliest times of the Church, was also reiterated most recently by Pope John Paul II in his apostolic exhortation, *Reconciliation and Penance*. Besides tradition, there are profound reasons for this way of administering the sacrament. Since all sin is an individual and personal act, it is most fitting that the confession of sins also be individual and personal. Jesus Christ is the Person who truly addresses the sinner and forgives him, as he did to the paralytic who had been brought to him by his friends. He said to him: **"My son, your sins are forgiven"** (Mk 2:5). We also think of the father in the parable of the prodigal son who personally extends himself to his son and forgives him, after his son's act of contrition. For this reason personal confession of sins is the only ordinary way that sins are forgiven in the Sacrament of Penance.

Penance may also take place as a communal celebration in which there is a series of common prayers and invocations, along with an examination of conscience. This highlights the ecclesial character of the sacrament, though the personal confession of sins and individual absolution should always be included as part of the liturgy. Often these communal penance services are organized in Advent or Lent by a parish or even a group of parishes, where several priests serve as confessors. It is a good opportunity not only to show solidarity with our brother priests, but to help the faithful to prepare as a community for the great feasts of the liturgical year.

In cases of grave necessity, a priest can impart *general absolution* after a general confession of sins. Such grave necessity could be the case of an imminent danger of death, without the opportunity for the people to confess their sins individually, or the case of people who would be deprived of sacramental forgiveness for a long time because of the shortage of priests—in mission territories, for instance. With respect to general absolution and confession, the *Catechism* (1483), citing Canon Law, also states that for the general absolution to be valid the faithful must have the intention of individually confessing their grave sins as soon as possible afterwards. The priest, as best as he can in the circumstances, should inform the faithful of this obligation, ask them to examine their consciences and make an act of contrition for their sins. For cases outside of imminent danger of death, the *Catechism* also states that the diocesan bishop is the one who should judge whether or not there are the conditions to give general absolution, and that a large gathering of faithful because of a feast or pilgrimage does not constitute a case of grave necessity.

You may wish to review the current rite of Penance for the Church as established by the Second Vatican Council, the *Ordo Paenitentiae*. It includes the rites for reconciliation of individual penitents, for that of several penitents with individual confession and absolution, and for that of penitents with general confession and absolution. Though in this Guidebook we refer to all three rites, we have concentrated above all on the penitent-confessor relationship which is present in the first two forms. We recommend that you review each of the rites carefully, especially the first and second ones which you will normally use. In accord with the Council's wishes, each of the revised rites includes a greater use of Scripture for the sacrament, and highlights the ecclesial nature of reconciliation.

Section III

Catechizing our People on the Need for Confession

Many of the faithful have an idea of sin that is not based on the Gospel but on common convention, on what is "socially acceptable." This makes them feel not particularly responsible for things that "everybody does," and all the more if these things are permitted by law. . . . Evangelization in the third millennium must come to grips with the urgent need for a presentation of the Gospel message which is dynamic, complete, and demanding. The Christian life to be aimed at cannot be reduced to a mediocre commitment to "goodness" as society defines it; it must be a true quest for holiness.

— POPE JOHN PAUL II, LETTER TO PRIESTS
ON HOLY THURSDAY, 2001, NO. 15

People today are deeply hurting because of sin, though they may not realize it. Habits of greed, selfishness, and lust can attach to them through others' lifestyles or their own weaknesses. As a result they are not happy with themselves, but often do not know why. They may even be good-hearted people, honest and personable in their dealings with others, but they are handicapped morally and spiritually—since they are confused about what is right or wrong, and have never seriously examined their conscience. They may have guilt feelings, but they are often of the kind imposed upon them by their friends or by political correctness, as in the case of the woman who feels very guilty about throwing a piece of paper on a lawn, or smoking in front of a child. But deeper questions such as her relationship with God, her friendships, the direction of her thoughts, or her sexual behavior never occur to her.

Somehow, Father, you and I have the mission to reach people like this and bring them to God, giving them his truth, and offering to them the great sacrament of forgiveness and hope.

Teaching about Sin and Virtue

Because of the blurring of the sense of sin in the modern world, we will need to preach about sin in our homilies or sermons, if not always then at least frequently. Don't feel that you are being judgmental or "pre-Vatican II" if you do this; it's your duty as the good shepherd of your people. If necessary, start a catechesis on this subject at your parish or school,[1] which could include the following elements:

1. A study of the Ten Commandments, with the corresponding virtues and sins which each one enjoins;

2. A description of the principal virtues connected with the natural law such as prudence, justice, temperance, and fortitude. (By speaking of the virtues first, in an encouraging and positive way, you will give people the right goals and standards for their lives; in this way also they can understand better how sin truly hurts them and their families.)

3. A description of the theological virtues infused into the soul at Baptism—faith, hope, and charity—along with the various sins against them such as willful dissent against the Church's teachings, superstitions, despair, presumption, indifference, and lukewarmness towards God.

In speaking about sin you must not think that you are being negative or mean-spirited; rather you are serving your people in a

---

[1] For this catechesis I recommend a book entitled *Looking for Peace? Try Confession*, by Mary Ann Budnik. (R.B. Media, Springfield, IL., 1997: now available at *www.rbmediainc.com.*) Besides giving an insightful description of the Sacrament of Confession and the good that it does for the soul, the first seven chapters deal with common objections or "hang ups" that modern Catholics could have with Confession, answering each of them in an informative and engaging way. For instance, "Why go to Confession if I can tell my sins directly to God?" or "Why examine my conscience, if I know that God is not legalistic?" or "Why go to Confession, since I have no mortal sins?" The book also has an appendix with examination of conscience questions for children and teens based on their particular situations.

most important and vital way. You are helping them to know the law and the love of God better, which in fact always go together; like the good shepherd, you are helping them to avoid acts and habits that will hurt their souls, and often their bodies.

During your catechesis be sure to explain clearly what constitutes a mortal sin, that is, the kind of sin that takes away sanctifying grace from the soul, and makes the person an enemy of God. For the good of their souls, the Church obliges Catholics to confess any mortal sins they have committed at least once a year (cf. *Code of Canon Law* [CIC], 989 and *Catechism of the Catholic Church* [CCC], 1457). If Catholics are conscious of any unconfessed mortal sins on their souls, they should not go to Communion, for this would be a sacrilege. As priests we may have to say this a number of times, since many may find it hard to believe, or even to admit that they could have committed a grave sin, at least materially. Mortal sin not only refers to hatred of God or direct rejection of him, but it can be any grave offense against his Law. In your explanation be sure to speak of the three elements involved in a grave sin: serious matter, sufficient reflection, and deliberate consent. It would also be helpful to give specific examples of mortal sins. Many Catholics today have never heard about them, or think that only certain evil people in history have committed them. They also need to have a clear description of what constitutes a venial sin. All of this is covered in *CCC* 1849–1864. The following section, entitled the *Proliferation of Sin* (*CCC* 1865 to 1869), would also be helpful to cover, since it speaks of the structures of sin in society, the so-called capital sins, and cooperation in sin, which can affect many people's lives.

This basic catechesis has for its purpose to heighten people's awareness of sin and thus the need for God's mercy in the Sacrament of Confession. If you as their priest or pastor do not tell them these things, they will either never hear of them, or if they do hear of sins, they will be distorted versions of morality drawn from unreliable sources. Recall also that you must be a father to them, who wants their good; a responsible father tells his children about what is right and wrong, and encourages them to live virtuous lives.

The Seven Capital Sins and their Opposing Virtues

In order to assist you in your instruction, and in helping people to form their consciences properly, we present a brief description of the seven capital sins. These are central flaws in human nature distinguished by the great theologians over the centuries; they result from original sin and from our fallen nature, and which account for most other sins.

- *Pride*, or excessive absorption with oneself and one's own excellence;
- *Gluttony*, the disordered attachment to food or drink and its pleasures;
- *Avarice*, the excessive desire for material goods;
- *Lust*, the disordered attachment to sexual pleasure;
- *Anger*, excessive frustration before difficulties;
- *Envy*, resentment of another's success or good fortune;
- *Sloth*, resistance or passivity before doing what is good or right.

We notice that the first four faults originate in something basically good. For instance, there is a good self-love, since persons and human nature are good in themselves; there is a legitimate attraction to food and drink for our own survival and health; there is the legitimate desire for sexual experience within marriage for the good of the couple, and for the engendering of children; there is a legitimate desire for material things as a means for perfecting our existence. But sin distorts the good purpose and use of our own bodies and the things around us, making them objects of selfishness or mere pleasure. The other three faults—anger, envy, and slothfulness—have to do with unjust or disordered reactions to persons or things.

The capital sins lead to other sins. For instance, pridefulness can easily lead to boasting, vanity, and scorn for others. It can even ally itself with shyness, since the proud person does not want to be seen with any faults. Its opposing virtue is **humility**, which the good priest confessor will know how to foster within the penitent.

Gluttony can lead not only to ill-health, but also to a certain dullness of mind and spirit that makes it more difficult to pray and to lead a life of virtue. Its opposing virtue is **temperance**. Lust can lead to spiritual blindness and even denial of the faith, since it often affects a person's power to reason and to see the truth about other people and things. It can also lead to disease and neglect of one's work and family. There is an epidemic of pornography on the Internet today that particularly affects men, which the good priest confessor must know about, along with the strong remedies needed. Lust also leads to impure acts alone or with others, such as premarital sex, masturbation, sodomy, and contraception. Its opposing virtue is **chastity** or **purity**. Greed or avarice can lead to stealing, fraud, and other forms of dishonesty. It also distracts a person from a life of prayer and friendship with others. Its opposing virtue is **detachment** or **generosity**. Anger can lead to cursing, spitefulness, and violence. It sometimes has its roots in suppressed feelings of frustration that can go back to childhood, and can be a cause of depression in some cases. Its opposing virtue is **forgiveness** or **kindness**. Envy can lead to stealing, gossiping, and even violence. Its opposing virtue is **gratitude** or **magnanimity**. Slothfulness often leads to the omission of one's duties at Church or in the home. It can affect one's basic attitude towards life and others, since it is essentially a kind of sadness or passivity when faced with the effort for doing good (called *acedia* in classical moral theology). Its opposing virtue is **optimism** or **industriousness**.

Such a catechesis on the capital sins, far from being depressing or negative, can really be liberating for people, since it will help them to know themselves better and to face their faults honestly, by giving a name to them. By identifying and understanding their weaknesses, they are more able to conquer them with God's help and their own efforts. It also helps the priest himself. If he knows how to examine his conscience humbly and sincerely in all of the above areas, and knows himself well, he will see evidence of these faults in his own life and soul. This is really a positive thing, since it will help him to be both a better confessor and penitent.

What the Penitent Should Do

Though this book is a guidebook for priests who are confessors, it is most helpful for your penitents to know how to make a good confession. Your role is to help your people learn how to make a sincere and complete confession, and to know the components of it. For this reason your instruction to your people should include a description of what happens in the Sacrament of Confession, and how Christ's infinite mercy comes into us.

Be sure to explain to them clearly what the penitent should do. To make a good confession the penitent needs to do four things: to examine his conscience well, to be sorry for his sins, to confess them humbly and sincerely, and to perform the prescribed penance.

A Good Examination of Conscience

To make a good examination of conscience, the person should think back over the time since his last good confession, and try to recall any sins or faults that he has committed. To aid him in this, he could go through the Ten Commandments, or consider the principal virtues of the Christian life, such as faith, hope, and charity—along with the moral virtues of prudence, justice, fortitude, and temperance. Some people have very good memories, or have a very sensitive awareness of their sins, and they may not have to spend much time in examining their consciences. Others, who have not been to confession in a long while, or who are making their first confession, may be helped by reading an examination of conscience that goes through the Ten Commandments, in question form, and gives the steps for making a good confession and the act of contrition. Try to have a good supply of these examinations of conscience to give to people. Make sure, of course, that they have proper ecclesiastical approval, and particularly that they cover the graver sins against the commandments or the moral and Christian virtues.

The main point of the examination of conscience is that people take the time to examine their behavior sincerely, and try to get to the root of their faults. Since confession is not a mere "laundry list" of sins—to use a very worn term—they should try to see the causes of their sins. For instance, a man who confesses the sin of anger with his family may find at the root of his anger a kind of pridefulness or unwillingness to forgive. A person who is lazy and neglects her duties at home may find at the root of that behavior a real lack of faith or hope in the graces of her Matrimony. The person who continually gossips at work may find, with closer examination, that he is really envious of others, or does not truly apply himself to his work. By getting to the root of his faults, therefore, a person can truly prepare himself for a more fruitful confession, and receive a greater amount of grace for overcoming his faults.

If you have a Catholic school, you could read a simple examination of conscience before the time for confessions.

Contrition for Sins

Once he has made a good examination of conscience—or even as he is making it—the sincere penitent should manifest his sorrow to God. Be sure to remind your people of this often, or else confession could become a mere mechanical listing of sins for some of them. As said above, this sorrow does not have to be emotional or expressed in tears, but it should include a clear recognition of the sinful actions they have committed—and the roots of those sins if possible—with a firm purpose of avoiding them in the future. This recognition and purpose of amendment are necessary for a valid confession. The sorrow that the person has may be perfect or imperfect. **Perfect contrition** is sorrow because of God's love for him, and because his sin has offended that love and kindness; **imperfect contrition** is sorrow because of the fear of suffering due to sin, either in Purgatory or in Hell. Imperfect contrition is sufficient for a valid confession and the forgiveness of sins, but the penitent should try—with the help of God's grace—to make his contrition more perfect, for instance, by reciting the act of perfect contrition. Its classical formulation is as follows: *O my God, I am heartily sorry for having offended thee, and I detest all my sins because I dread the loss of heaven and the pains of hell. But most of all because they have offended thee, my God, who art all good and deserving of all my love. I firmly resolve, with the help of thy grace, to confess my sins, to do penance, and to amend my life. Amen.* Though the quality of a person's contrition cannot be determined by a formula alone, you may wish to ask your people—both young and older—to learn the classical act of contrition which they can say before receiving the sacrament, or even, if they wish, at the proper moment within confession.

If the person doesn't know the act of contrition, or has forgotten it, you can always suggest one to them, or even say it with them if they are nervous. Perhaps a simple one, like "Jesus, Son of God, have mercy on me, a sinner," would be appropriate, since it has more Scriptural foundations.

When you're hearing confessions, remember that for the good of his soul, and for the validity of the sacrament, the penitent should confess any unconfessed mortal sins in number and specific kind that he has discovered in his examination of conscience (see Council of Trent, sess. XIV, chapter 5, and also the *Code of Canon Law*, c. 988 no. 1). This is the necessary matter to make a good confession. Until he confesses these sins, he should refrain from receiving Holy Communion, as said above. If there is a grave reason for receiving Communion, he should ask God for the grace and try to make an act of perfect contrition, with the purpose of going to individual confession as soon as possible (see *CIC* 916). You can help him to overcome any kind of fear or shame in confessing these sins, by reminding him that he is not confessing them to you, but to the Most Merciful and Sacred Heart of Christ. This confession of grave sins guarantees the integrity of the confession, and also demonstrates the humility and sorrow of the penitent.

To confess grave sins in number and specific kind means that the person must be detailed enough for you the priest, who is a merciful judge as well as a loving father at that moment, to understand clearly what sins the persons actually committed, and the state of the person's soul—in order to give an appropriate penance and the best advice. Therefore, if the person is confessing a sin against justice or the seventh commandment, it would not be enough for him to say "I have sinned against justice, or I have sinned against the seventh commandment." He should also state the kind of sin it was—for instance, stealing, destruction of property, cheating—and the harm that was done to another, whether grave or slight. It is certainly different to steal 25 cents than to steal $250. It is also different to steal $20 from a very poor person than to steal the same amount from a rich person. In cases of injustice, you should also make sure that the penitent is willing to make some kind of restitution for the sin, either right away or in time, for this is an intrinsic demand of true sorrow and purpose of amendment.

Although venial sins can be forgiven in other ways such as acts of penance and the reception of Holy Communion, it is recommended that the penitent include venial sins in his confession (see *CCC* 1458). Be sure to include this in your catechesis, and list for them the great benefits of this practice: the penitent can be sure that his venial sins are truly forgiven; temporal punishment due to them is reduced or taken away; he will receive a specific grace to avoid them in the future; he can receive advice on how to avoid or diminish them in his life; he can avoid mortal sins more easily; his conscience becomes more refined as he confesses them.

Frequent confession is also highly recommended. Even if a person has not committed any grave sins, he receives a grace to improve in his life and to become more and more like Christ. Frequent confession helps a person to grow in humility, to combat any possible lukewarmness and, as said above, to develop a more refined and sensitive conscience as he examines his actions more frequently, and receives good advice from the confessor. It also helps a person to have more trust in God and grow in devotion to the Most Just and Merciful Heart of Christ, and to experience the great peace that a good confession will bring.

Qualities of a Good Confession

The qualities of a good confession, which you will need to facilitate in some cases, can be summarized with the four "c's" It should be **concise**, that is, without circumlocutions or excuses. It should be **concrete,** that is, avoiding generalities and giving the number and specific kind of sin. It should be **clear,** so that you know what sins are being confessed, and any circumstances making the sin more serious or less serious. It should be **complete**, so that all unconfessed mortal sins are mentioned in number and in kind. If the person is not able to give the exact number of times, he can give an approximation, or simply say "many times" or "few times" as he can best remember.

Related to the four "c's" are the virtues of humility and honesty. A person does not go to confession to chat with the priest about other matters, or to discuss other people's sins. The purpose of the sacrament is to confess his or her own sins humbly, in order to receive God's forgiveness and to listen to the priest's advice. If the person needs to discuss related matters, or the faults of others that affect his life, perhaps you could suggest that he make an appointment to speak of these things in spiritual direction or counseling, or the person himself could give a little explanation of his situation to you before his confession.

Fulfilling the Penance

To do penance for sins is the fourth act of the penitent. It is his way of showing God that he is truly sorry for his sins, and that he is willing to perform extra prayers or good works in order to make up for them. This is also called *satisfaction*. Satisfaction is related to atonement, for by connecting a prayer or good work to the paschal mystery of Christ, the penitent in some way *makes up* for his sins before God, and gives clear evidence of his sorrow. The word satisfaction actually comes from the two Latin words "*satis facere*," which literally mean *to do enough*. But this must be understood in the right way. Since sin is in some way infinite because an Infinite Person has been offended, our satisfaction can only take place through the satisfaction offered by the infinite Person of Christ and his sacrifice on Calvary. Because of this, it is true to say that no human being by his efforts alone can do enough to atone for even one venial sin.

The penitent should do the penance as soon as possible. If it is a particularly long or difficult penance, he can speak with the priest about it, or if the priest insists on it and he thinks that he is unable to fulfill it, he is free to go to confession with another priest. If he fails to fulfill a penance for whatever reason, he should bring this up in his next confession, but this does not invalidate his previous confession as long as he had the intention of performing the penance at the time he received it.

Though penitents are not bound by the seal of confession, they do have the natural obligation of confidentiality not to mention things spoken to him in confession that could harm the priest or the sacrament itself, for the priest cannot defend himself.

Temporal Punishment and Indulgences

Be sure to tell your people that while a sincere confession forgives the guilt of mortal and venial sins, there may still be some temporal punishment due for them. **Temporal punishment** is due for sin because of the disordered attachment to sinful habits or desires that may still reside in our soul, even after our sins are forgiven. For instance if a man confesses angry outbursts with his wife, his sins are forgiven, but the tendency to anger may still continue within him, if it is a habit. The same applies to other kinds of sin, for instance of pride or impurity. In order for our souls to be completely purified and to reach Eternal Happiness, those attachments need to be purified and removed. The satisfaction that we accept and carry out after confession removes some of this punishment, but the rest of it needs to be removed by penance, prayer, and good works in this life, or in Purgatory.

The Church in her merciful love for us can draw from the treasury of the satisfaction and merits of Christ and the saints, and apply these graces to us for the remission of temporal punishment. These merits applied to us are called **indulgences**, and we can obtain them by performing certain good works, such as prayers and sacrifices, under certain conditions. A plenary indulgence takes away all the temporal punishment due to sin, a partial indulgence takes away some of it.

It would be most helpful and charitable to speak frequently to your people about temporal punishment and indulgences. Many people have never heard of them, or only have vague ideas about them. Individuals and families can receive great benefits for their souls by gaining indulgences for themselves and others—particularly the souls in Purgatory—by performing certain works and devotions throughout the year, including the Way of the Cross, the family Rosary, and visits to the Blessed Sacrament.[2]

A Few Particular Cases

As said above, you should always try to help the person to make an integral confession, which will include any unconfessed mortal sins that he or she is capable of confessing at that moment, but there may be serious reasons that could excuse the penitent from making an integral confession, or the priest from hearing one. These are:

1. Physical impossibility, such as the inability to speak due to illness, unconsciousness, or other causes. Of course if the person can communicate by writing, through sign language or through an interpreter, this is permitted, but the interpreter will then be bound by the seal of confession;

2. The danger of scandal or sin, on the part of the penitent or confessor. That is, if the penitent states something, or the confessor asks a certain question, this may lead to grave physical or spiritual harm either for the penitent or the minister;

---

[2] See *CCC* 1471–1479; Also Pope Paul VI, Apostolic Constitution *Indulgentiarum Doctrina*, January 1, 1967.

3. The possibility of breaking the seal of confession by what is asked or stated;

4. The danger of revealing the identity of an accomplice in sin, or the taking away of one's own good name and that of other persons. This can happen in communities where everyone knows each other well.

General Confession as a Need

If the penitent has deliberately hidden a grave sin that he should have confessed, or given an ambiguous or false answer to the confessor when all the conditions were present for him to make an integral confession, he will have to confess that grave sin at the next confession, along with any other grave sins that he may have committed after the bad confession. In some cases, if the person made a bad confession some time before, and never confessed the hidden sin, he will have to make a general confession covering that time; that is, he will have to confess the grave sin that he hid, along with any bad confessions that he may have made afterwards, and any grave sins that he committed after the first bad confession, since none of them were forgiven.

In these cases be sure to be very compassionate and encouraging, and help the person through his general confession. First, you should tell him the reason for confessing these sins again, so that he will not think that you are being overly curious or severe. For instance, you could say, "By hiding that sin you have made your subsequent confessions questionable—to say the least. This is the perfect time to thoroughly clear up the past, so you can truly put it behind you. To ensure that, let me help you with a general confession."

If a person simply forgot to confess a grave sin in confession, and did not deliberately withhold it, he should mention it in his next confession, along with other sins that he may have committed since his last confession.

General Confession as a Devotion

General confession can be a very good devotional practice also. For instance, a person may wish to confess the sins of his past life before a big and important event in his life, such as his marriage, or the reception of Holy Orders, or at a retreat. If he has no past bad confession on his soul, he can make the general confession as he wishes: that is, by simply confessing in a general way his sins against certain virtues or commandments, for instance: "I'm sorry for my past sins against charity; I'm sorry for my past sins against purity." Or if he wishes, he may be more specific and confess those sins for which he's particularly sorry, or some of the circumstances behind them that made them more serious. This general confession provides a special sacramental grace and helps the person to begin anew in his struggle to become a saint. As the priest taking care of a sick or elderly person in the final months of his life, you can also recommend that he make a general confession, either separately or as part of the Anointing of the Sick.

Section IV

The Minister of the Sacrament of Forgiveness

Our Great Privilege as Priests Is to Bring Souls Closer to Jesus Christ

Of course all the sacraments are essential for doing this, particularly the Holy Eucharist, when we bring His Body and Blood to others, and reproduce his sacrifice on the altars. But the Sacrament of Confession in many ways is the most personal of all the sacraments for us, since we can enter more directly into the inner sanctum of a person, and bring Christ's grace of healing. As Saint John Eudes once said, "the preacher gives souls to God, and the confessor saves them." The words of absolution that we pronounce may often be the most comforting words that a man or woman can hear, and the counsel that we give can be life-changing. Above all, it is Christ himself working through us as Judge, Shepherd, Physician, and greatest Friend.

For this reason it is most helpful to prepare ourselves spiritually before we hear confessions, just as we should prepare ourselves before saying Mass or administering one of the other sacraments. We must realize that people will be revealing their souls and innermost thoughts to us, and entrusting themselves to our judgment in very important matters. In this way our hearing of confessions will never be a cause of distaste or scorn for souls, but should rather increase our honor and reverence for them, as we hear of their personal struggles and their desires to repent.

Though a Guidebook of this kind has to make certain generalizations, we as priest confessors should always remember that every individual is unique and precious in God's sight. No two confessions are ever the same, really, even though the same types of sin are repeated frequently. You must always remember that **a child of God** is before you—with virtues and defects, clear points and ambiguities—and that this child of God is called to become a saint, and to have the fullness of divine life in him or her. And you can generally presume that they have good will, since they have been humble enough to come to you to confess their sins, some of which could be quite embarrassing for them.

Praying before Hearing Confessions

As a result it is good to pray for a certain reverence, even *awe*, before every person who comes to confess to you—including children. Pray to the Holy Spirit, as the Holy Curé of Ars did, for the grace to understand and assist each person who comes to the sacrament. He or she should always feel welcomed and strengthened in their confession, even if you are tired and have already heard many confessions.

Perhaps a good prayer to recite before hearing confessions is this one addressed to the Holy Trinity: **"God the Father, may I be a Father; God the Son, may I judge according to your Most Merciful Heart; God the Holy Spirit, may I be a teacher, shepherd, and physician."** Since Saint John Marie Vianney, the Curé of Ars, is the patron saint of all diocesan priests, and spent so many years in the confessional doing immense good for others, and converting thousands, we could also invoke him with the following words: *"Saint John Marie, may I listen carefully to all those who come now to the sacrament. Help me to exercise the gift of discernment, so that I may grasp each person's situation, and give words of instruction, encouragement, and correction whenever needed—for the good of his or her soul. May I also pray and do penance for all those who confess their sins to God through me, so that I may be Christ's faithful minister on earth."*

Some priests also like to pray the traditional "Veni Creator" prayer to the Holy Spirit, remembering that confession is the Lord's Easter gift to his Church, as he imparted the Holy Spirit to the apostles on the day of his Resurrection (cf. Jn 20:22).

Receiving the Proper Faculties

Since the priest is really the collaborator of his bishop in each diocese, who is entrusted principally with the *cura animarum* and who is Christ's vicar, he must obtain his permission to hear confessions. This includes the proper reception of faculties which enables a priest to hear confessions validly in the bishop's jurisdiction, and to grant absolution for sins (see *Code of Canon Law* nos. 966 and 967). Normally all diocesan priests are given such faculties upon their ordination and incardination in the diocese. According to the new *Code*, other priests visiting the diocese are automatically granted such faculties if they have valid faculties from a bishop of another jurisdiction, and are in good standing. If a priest has been deprived of his faculties for whatever reason by his legitimate Ordinary, he does not have faculties in other dioceses. For the above reason, as good confessors we must always try to be united with the instructions and spiritual guidelines given by our bishop for the faithful of his diocese, and will instruct our people accordingly: in preaching, in spiritual direction, and in the Sacrament of Confession.

We Ourselves should Be Good Penitents

Of course for a priest to be a good confessor of souls, **he too should be a good penitent**. Pope John Paul II actually affirmed that if the priest himself was not regular in his own confessions, and did not receive Penance with a spirit of faith and devotion, his priesthood would suffer "an inexorable decline." (see Apostolic Exhortation *Reconciliatio et Poenitentia*, no. 31.VI). If a man is going to heal the frailties and weaknesses of others, it is most fitting that he know his own frailties and weaknesses, and himself be a frequent and humble recipient of Penance.

There are many temptations in the world today, which come from both inside and outside. As we make our examination of conscience as priests each night, we will naturally notice things that have not been right about our day. Perhaps we have put off or missed part of the Divine Office, or we have wasted time when we should have been working on our homilies or other parish matters. We may have been rude to a person at the rectory, or to a fellow priest. We may have given into gossip or negative conversations about fellow priests, or the bishop. We may have fallen into sadness or self-pity, forgetting the merciful love of Christ for us and of his Blessed Mother. Or we may have fallen into sins of sensuality—with the abuse of food or drink, or with faults against the sixth commandment, whether in thought, word, or action.

As soon as we are aware of our sins, let us make an immediate act of contrition, "as blood flowing to a wound," in the graphic expression of Saint Josemaría Escrivá. And with our act of contrition of course should come a purpose of amendment. In this way we will be anxious for our day of confession. I recommend that this be once a week for all priests, with a regular confessor or spiritual director who knows us well and can help us with our recurring faults. Of course as faithful of the Church we have the right to go to confession with whomever we wish, as long as he has valid faculties, but it is better for our souls if we have a fixed confessor or spiritual director, who can help us in an ongoing way.

A priest must go to confession as soon as possible if he has committed grave sin, not only for the good of his soul, but to celebrate the other sacraments worthily, especially the Holy Eucharist. This is also the case with the hearing of confessions; his soul should be in the state of grace, though this is not necessary for the validity of the sacrament. As in the celebration of the Mass, he may have to hear confessions in the state of grave sin for the good of souls, but he should try to make an act of perfect contrition, asking God's grace to do so, and then get to confession as soon as possible.

Even in the case of venial sins or other faults and imperfections, it is most recommended that the priest go to confession frequently. In this way he not only receives sacramental grace to improve in virtue, but his conscience becomes more refined in order to hear the confessions of others with greater insight, and to exercise more effectively his ministry of judge, shepherd, and physician of hearts.

Pope John Paul II beautifully summarized the above points in his 2001 Holy Thursday Letter to Priests (no. 11):

> Dear Priests, let us make regular use of this Sacrament, that the Lord may constantly purify our hearts and make us less unworthy of the mysteries which we celebrate. Since we are called to show forth the face of the Good Shepherd, and therefore to have the heart of Christ himself, we more than others must make our own the Psalmist's ardent cry: "A pure heart create for me, O God, put a steadfast spirit within me." (Ps 51:12) The Sacrament of Reconciliation, essential for every Christian life, is especially a source of support, guidance and healing for the priestly life.

Fidelity and Formation of the Priest Confessor

Since the priest exercises his ministry within the Mystical Body of Christ, and since Penance is a sacrament by the Church and for the Church, we must have a clear understanding of the Church's teachings, especially in matters of faith and morals. These teachings have been preserved and communicated through the Magisterium of the Church from her very beginning. As the Lord said to his apostles, **"All authority in heaven and on earth has been given to me. Go therefore and make disciples of all nations. . . . teaching them to observe all that I have commanded you"** (Mt 27:19–20). And to emphasize the continuity between his disciples' teachings and his own, he also stated: **"He who hears you, hears me; and he who rejects you, rejects me, and he who rejects me rejects him who sent me"** (Lk 10:16). If a priest has not carefully studied the Church's teachings, especially those related to morality and the life of virtue, he should not enter the confessional, since he runs the serious risk of misleading those individuals who come to him. Even more so, if a priest knowingly dissents from the Magisterium on issues of faith and morals, he is obliged not to hear confessions. The dissent or ambiguity of many priests on the matter of contraception and other sins against the sixth commandment has been very harmful for the Church in the last forty years; the spiritual damage to individuals and families has been immense. The same may be said, to a lesser degree, on the Church's teachings about human life and its dignity.

The Best Ways of Acting and Speaking in the Confessional

As said above, the priest must be a judge, shepherd, physician, and father for all those who approach him for reconciliation. To be all four of these requires a great deal of humility, sufficient learning, and a lot of prayer and common sense. Because every priest is a man who also suffers from original sin—which includes vanity, prideful reactions, and superficiality—he should examine his words and way of acting in the confessional frequently, so that he be truly an effective minister of Christ. He should not be content simply to impart a valid absolution; he must impart it through the mind and heart of Christ, who is the Merciful Judge of all mankind. In the same way, his advice, correction, and encouragement should be as close as possible to that advice, correction, and encouragement which the Savior himself would impart to the man, woman, or child who confess their sins to him.

Of course he should avoid anything in his tone of voice or comments that could sound abrupt or sarcastic. He should not interrupt the penitent, but if necessary, ask the right kind of question at the right time. He should not give the impression that he is merely curious about things, or tell jokes—though at times he could use a bit of humor perhaps to help a tense penitent to relax and be more sincere. Above all he should never lose his temper or became impatient with penitents, though he may be tired and have a large number of people in line. There have been cases, sadly, of people who have left the Church because of the bad temper or ill-considered remarks of priests in the confessional.

As a matter of fact, the confessional should really be *a place of joy for the penitent*. It is not easy to kneel down and manifest the ugliness of one's soul to a fellow mortal; but a complete and sincere confession will invariably produce an experience of relief and happiness—that of beginning life again with the confidence of being loved, forgiven, and supported. **For this reason the priest must never give the impression that he is tired or does not like to hear confessions.** While his time may be brief with each one because of the line of people waiting, each penitent should have the impression that Father is happy to spend this needed time with them, and that he sincerely cares for them and wants them to be happy in their lives. Ultimately, it is God's grace that brings the greatest joy to a person, knowing that they are back in their Heavenly Father's home. As Pope John Paul II states: *Every confessional is a special and blessed place from which, with divisions wiped away, there is born new and uncontaminated a reconciled individual—a reconciled world!*[1]

Though it may seem to be an external consideration only, I think it would be worthwhile to comment briefly on a *priest's posture* in receiving confessions. Of course one's posture in no way affects the validity of the sacrament; in times of emergency, like giving absolution to a person trapped in a mine, a priest may have to be lying down. At times he may have to be standing in a corner, or leaning over a hospital bed, or walking alongside of the penitent. But normally in a confessional or Reconciliation room he will be seated, and should maintain a posture which is both respectful and alert. Therefore the priest should not be slouching in the chair, or leaning his head against the confessional screen, but should try to keep both feet on the ground and maintain an erect position. The chair he uses should not be too hard, because this could be quite difficult if he has to hear many confessions, nor should it be too soft or comfortable, for this could limit his alertness or even lead to sleep. If there are spaces of time between confessions, a priest should not take naps, read the newspaper or some other secular publication, browse the Internet with a laptop, eat food or drink sodas, use his cell phone for calls, etc. He can use this period as a time of prayer, a holy time,

---

[1] John Paul II, Apostolic Exhortation *Reconciliatio et Poenitentia* (1984) n.31.V.

in which he can pray for more penitents, or for those whose confessions he has just heard. Other good uses of waiting time are to read a good theology or spiritual book, to say the Rosary or Chaplet of Divine Mercy, or pray the Divine Office.

The Priest as Judge, Shepherd, Physician, and Father

Let's consider each of these capacities carefully, since all of them are mentioned in the *Catechism of the Catholic Church* (cf. *CCC* 1465).

The good confessor is a judge. This can make some priests cringe, since it sounds like "being judgmental" which has very negative connotations for many today. In an age of subjectivism, to judge anyone is almost considered to be a grave sin. Yet it was the same Christ who told his apostles, upon giving them the power of absolution, "whose sins you shall forgive, they are forgiven them; whose sins you shall retain, they are retained." The granting of forgiveness certainly implies the duty and need for the confessor to make some kind of judgment about the gravity of the person's sin, and the state of the person's soul. If a priest cannot be a judge of these things in the name of Christ, he cannot give a true absolution to the person, since he has no idea of what he is absolving. Nor could he judge if the person is truly sorry and repentant for his or her sin, which is one of the essential conditions for absolution. He could also give no useful counsel, since he would have no idea of the person's real state of soul. But since the priest must also be a man of compassion who brings people the mercy of Christ, perhaps a good way to look at the priest as confessor is to say that he is indeed a judge, but **a judge according to the mind and heart of Christ**.

The good confessor is also a shepherd. He must learn to lead people to God through his instruction and encouragement, while removing them from danger, as a good shepherd will remove his sheep from the precipice or from wolves. This means that he must have a good grasp of the dangers that people face today—as indeed the priest himself faces—and how best to alert people to these dangers. At times he will have to repeat to them the rudiments of the Faith, especially regarding basic duties of prayer and virtue. At the same time he should always be in search of fresh and nourishing pastures for those entrusted to him: ways to form good habits of prayer and virtue which will bring people to true happiness. Like a good shepherd, at times he will have to bind up the wounds of people—whether caused by bad habits, by the aftermath of abuse or hatred, by psychological illness, or simply by loneliness. In some way he must take the person upon his shoulders and let him know that he is there for him, and that he will pray for him.

The good confessor is also a physician. He knows people, has studied moral theology, and can identify the principal spiritual ailments that people can suffer from: the pridefulness that blinds and can lead to isolation from God and others, or stubbornness in changing one's opinion; the lust that enslaves and weakens a person's capacity to believe and do good; the anger that disorients and hurts both the individual and her family. As a good physician he also knows how to ask the right questions so that he can get to the cause of the hurt or illness. At times he will have to perform a delicate surgery, after discovering the site of the infection or the wound, and with the help of God's grace, he can remove it by prompting the person to make a sincere confession of the sin and a good act of contrition; afterwards he binds up the wound with the salve of kindness and sound advice. At times his medicine will be more gradual and ongoing, as he helps people little by little to be more sincere and know themselves better, and to strengthen their practice of virtues such as patience, humility, and chastity.

The good confessor is also a father. It is not by chance that Pope John Paul II chose the parable of the prodigal son as the leading scriptural text of his apostolic exhortation on Penance. God is very much a Father who longingly awaits the arrival of his wayward son back home. He watches the horizon each day in search of him. And when he sees him come, he personally goes out to meet him. Not only does he not hold a grudge against his sinful son, but he forgives him generously, gives him a ring for his finger, and kills the fatted calf for a celebration (see Lk 15:22–23). Such is the role of the priest in confession, as the minister of the Father in Heaven. He must be truly delighted that people come to the sacrament—whether they come regularly or after a long time, though he will be particularly glad, of course, if they are coming back to confession after a long time away. He is truly desirous to receive each penitent back to his home, which is the Church and the Communion of Saints. The penitent in some way should sense this warmth in the priest's manner or tone of voice. He should not hear the cold and distant voice of a mere functionary of the Church in that moment, but the warm and hopeful voice of a loving father who is delighted at his child's conversion, and has many gifts to bestow upon him.

In all of the above capacities, the priest should know how to combine prudence and compassion. He must be prudent in that he understands what the penitent really needs in his or her condition of soul. He will not say too much so as to crush the person's spirit, nor blow out the tiny flame of conversion that at times is just barely lit. But he will not say too little, so as to leave a person ignorant of the basic truths he needs to know in order to be saved, or to progress in his spiritual life. He has the gift of compassion since he truly "suffers with" the person, though he must also have the good detachment of a physician who knows that he has many other penitents to heal, and confessions to hear. When a penitent goes to confession with such a priest, she will know that she is not only loved, but that she has been understood and given the best counsel for her situation. In a word, she will know that she has received forgiveness from Christ himself.

Punctuality and Availability

Continuing a description of a priest's role, he should of course be punctual and available for hearing confessions. The faithful must never get the impression that "father is too busy to hear your confession." At times this might require considerable sacrifice. The best approach is to establish generous and regular hours when people can go to confession. Some priests are available on weekdays before and after every Mass, which is very helpful for people. Many parishes have hours on Saturday afternoons, which seems like a convenient time for people, and a good way to help them to prepare for Sunday Mass. But in a big parish, just a half hour or forty-five minutes of confession time does not seem enough, let alone fifteen minutes. Perhaps if the parish is near an office or working district, confessions can be offered during the lunch hour, or the hours immediately after work.

The priest should never leave the confessional early just because only a few people come or nobody comes. Perhaps at first only a few grandmothers will come for confession, but in time, they'll bring their children and grandchildren! It may happen that a person comes in need of confession and the priest has already left. The confessional light, like the tabernacle light, shines as a living witness to the presence of the merciful Christ. If few people or nobody comes, you can take advantage of the time by saying the Rosary for people, or by good spiritual reading.

The main point is that the priest must be a father and a shepherd who is readily available for others, and they will appreciate it.

The Importance of an Integral Confession

One of our most important duties as priest confessors—very much connected with our role of judge, shepherd, physician, and father—is to help persons to make an integral confession. The *Ordo Paenitentiae* (no.18) states that if necessary the priest should help the penitent to do this, along with encouraging him to have sorrow for his sins, and to offer him suitable counsel and instruction. As said above, every penitent is obliged to confess any and all unconfessed mortal sins since his last worthy confession that he can recall after a good examination of conscience. An integral confession is not simply the saying of one sin or a "representative" sin at a penance service. It is not simply to write down a few things on paper. This abuse was pointed out clearly by the Congregation for Divine Worship and Discipline of the Sacraments.[2]

People with good formation in the Faith will normally be able to make an integral confession of their sins—but given the poor education of so many souls in the Faith, especially in the commandments and the moral law, we will often have to ask the pertinent questions to help a person say all that he or she should say.[3] These should always been done in a discreet and moderate way—explaining to the person that we would like to ask a few questions to help with the completeness of the confession, and to help the person form his conscience better. The wise old Latin refrain says that the priest in speaking to souls should be "*suaviter in modo, fortiter in re.*" He should be gentle in his words and manner, but strong in the truth.

A typical case would be that of an individual who has been away for many months or years from confession, and only confesses in a very general and summary way—for instance that he has been "unloving," or that he has done things "that he is not proud of," but without saying much else. At this point we could request his permission to ask a few questions, just in case he may have forgotten something, since his last confession was a long time ago. Then we should patiently go through the commandments or the basic moral and theological virtues with the person—teaching gently all the time, and even apologizing for the time taken, but assuring him that in this way the confession will be truly complete and pleasing to God—and of greater benefit for himself. In almost all cases the penitent will be happy to comply; after all, he has come to the sacrament to be cleansed, and the priest is simply helping him to make a complete confession.

---

[2] See *Circular Letter Concerning the Integrity of the Sacrament of Penance*, n.6 issued by the above Congregation on March 20, 2000.

[3] As said earlier, it is most helpful to give the person a simple guide for making a good confession, with some basic questions about the virtues and commandments, and the necessary dispositions of contrition. But even in this case the priest should listen carefully, and may have to ask pertinent questions.

Prudence and Refinement in Asking

In asking persons about their sins, we of course must be prudent and delicate, but we must not fear to get to the truth. Often, at least over the past forty years, many Catholics have not heard of mortal sin, nor the obligation to attend Mass on Sunday, nor the possibility of receiving Communion unworthily, nor the gravity of sins against the sixth commandment. Many may not even know what are the sixth commandment, or the virtue of chastity. In the case of invincible ignorance, of course, the person is not guilty of formal sin, but when he goes to confession we have an excellent opportunity to instruct him on the basic principles of the moral law—by asking the right questions, and explaining things clearly, even if the time is brief.

In the case of married persons, and especially if they have been away from confession for a long time, we need to ask if he or she is open to children in their marital relations. If they are limiting the number of children, we can discreetly inquire about the reasons for the decision, and the means they are using. We should let them know that the only legitimate ways to limit children is either through abstinence or natural family planning. The so-called contraceptive pills, besides being contraceptives, are abortofacient in many cases. We will speak more of this later in the section on chastity.

In hearing confessions of spouses, we must be careful not to use specific information or data from the other spouse's confession in asking questions or giving counsel. This could produce resentment and misunderstanding, and even constitute an indirect violation of the seal. If we are patient and know how to ask in the right way about their relationship, we will be able to help both of them.

There are certain occasions when we can simply ask in general about marital duties, for instance, in the confessions of persons with very little formation or intelligence, of persons going to their children's wedding or first communion and do not want to give scandal by not receiving Communion, of older persons, who are beyond the age for having children. Nevertheless we must always clarify grave matters if they come up in confession; the person should not leave with material ignorance about what is right or wrong.

The confessor at times will have to instruct the penitent in some basic truths of the Faith, if they are deficient in their knowledge or practice of them. As the confession proceeds, he may also have to form the conscience of the person, explaining briefly why some things are right or wrong, while avoiding any tone of arguing. In other words, the priest, as another Christ, truly takes upon himself the dispositions, struggles, and failures of the penitent, while giving appropriate and positive advice, and helping the penitent to leave with a firm purpose of amendment and confident that God's grace will help him or her.

Proportionate and Helpful Penances

In general the penance should fit the gravity and number of the sins confessed. If the sins are grave, the penance should be greater; if they are light, the penance should be lighter. Examples of more serious penances would be to go to Mass during the week, to fast, to say a complete Rosary, or a decade of the Rosary on one's knees. Devout people will accept these penances readily, and even be open for harder ones—but for other souls these penances might be too difficult, and the priest should be aware of this. In this case he may give a lighter penance, such as the saying of three Hail Mary's, but then he himself, as another Christ, can perform a supplementary penance to make atonement for the sins confessed to him.

Upon occasion we will notice that a person has mixed motives in confession, or, from the tone of voice or other evidence, it may seem that he or she is not truly sorry for their sins. At other times it might seem that some people, including children, are merely giving a list of sins, but with little desire of amendment. In these cases we must help them to see the evil of sin, and move them to repentance as best we can, while invoking the grace of the Holy Spirit. We could even ask them questions such as "Which sin are you most sorry for?" or "How do you think you can avoid that sin in the future?" By asking these things, we can help people to think about their souls and their life in ways that they have not done before.

Only after applying all the means does the priest have grounds for denying absolution; that is, if the person shows no sign of remorse, or refuses to avoid an occasion of grave sin, or at least try to break from a sinful habit. The best thing however, if at all possible, is not to deny absolution; if someone is not truly penitent, or not in condition to receive absolution for some other reason, the best thing is to *postpone* the absolution, while asking the person to read something or pray about something in the meantime. This leaves the door open to his or her coming back to the sacrament. Some situations can be complex; for instance a person may want to break from a bad situation, but recognizes his weaknesses and knows it will be easy for him to fall again. In this case, the priest should still give absolution, encouraging him to return to confession as often as necessary, in order to obtain God's grace. Not everything can be resolved at once, but the penitent should at least recognize his or her fault, and be willing to use the means to overcome it.

In the case of people suffering from an accident or in an unconscious condition, the priest should speak into the ear of the person, inviting him to make an act of contrition; then he should pronounce clearly the words of absolution, in an absolute way if he shows signs of awareness and contrition, or in a conditional way, if this is doubtful. Some people may actually be alert and understanding, but unable to speak. In these cases, the priest, with a little bit of ingenuity, can go through the commandments or principal Christian virtues, and ask the person to blink his eye if he is guilty of some sin, or squeeze the priest's hand as he asks questions, signifying that the answer is yes. If a person has died only shortly before the priest arrives, he can give a conditional absolution and anointing,[4] after speaking into the person's ear and inviting him to make an act of contrition.

How to Deal with Recidivists and Other Similar Cases

People who live in the occasion of sin are obliged to remove themselves from that occasion; for instance the man who has a

---

[4] McHugh-Callan, *Moral Theology Vol. II* (New York: Joseph F. Wagner, Inc., 1958), page 740.

weakness for alcohol should not walk down a street that has bars on it. However there may be some cases in which a person must remain within an occasion of sin, for instance, a book store employee who may see bad magazines in the store, a secretary who is surrounded by people who continually gossip, a student whose friends bring pornographic pictures to school, etc. In such cases the penitent must do all he can to make the occasion remote, and to show in confession his willingness to do so. There may be some cases, however, where the environment is so bad that the person will have to quit that kind of work and look for other employment, or take strong measures such as speaking to someone in authority about the situation.

Recidivists are those who have a habit of sinning gravely, and who cannot seem to overcome it. They come to confession often, but they fall again into the same sins.

If they are not truly sorry or are not struggling against the sin, in principle the confessor should not give them absolution. But he should also keep two things in mind. First, if the habit is very strong, the penitent may have less freedom of choice in order to avoid it, and in this case it would not be a grave sin for him. And second, the mere fact of coming to confession shows repentance and desire to begin again. Therefore it is probably better to give absolution in these cases, and if necessary, to err on the side of mercy rather than to refuse absolution. But we must make sure that the person is truly struggling against this habit, to avoid his abusing the grace of the sacrament.

The Absolution of Censures and other Canonical Penalties

For the good priest confessor, the Church's laws are not simply mechanical rules or regulations that burden one's mind or soul. Since the Church is a society established by Christ for the good of souls, she has the right and duty to establish certain laws and determine penalties in order to carry out her supernatural mission, just as civil governments have the right to establish laws to protect the common good. For this reason the priest confessor must be aware of those areas of Canon Law that affect his penitents, so that he can give the proper advice and remedies to those coming to him, and to assure their full reconciliation with the Church.

Please check **Appendix II** for a more detailed description of these Canon Law requirements.

Section V

The Obligation of the Confessor
after Confession

Though a person's sins are forgiven through God's merciful love, and the merits of Jesus Christ, it is praiseworthy for a priest to make acts of reparation for the sins that he has heard, and even to make up by his own prayers or sacrifices what is lacking as far as penance. The Holy Curé of Ars would spend hours on his knees after hearing some confessions, making up in his flesh for the sins of others—similar to Christ's own action on the cross. To a fellow priest the Curé once explained: *"I will tell you my recipe: I give sinners a small penance and the rest I do in their place."*[1]

It is hard to say the degree of obligation that priests have to make extra reparation for the sins they hear—for these have truly been forgiven by Christ in the sacrament—but such acts of penance and atonement are highly recommended for the priest confessor, and can help take away the penitent's temporal punishment due to those sins. Let us never forget that a priest is *alter Christus*, another Christ, and that he should bring Christ's own dispositions on the cross for the good of souls.

Commenting on the penance and spirit of reparation that Saint John Marie Vianney possessed, Pope Benedict declared the following in his Letter proclaiming a Year for Priests (June 2009): *Aside from the actual penances which the Curé of Ars practiced, the core of his teaching remains valid for each one of us: souls have been won at the price of Jesus' own blood, and a priest cannot devote himself to their salvation if he refuses to share personally in the "precious cost" of redemption.*

---

[1] Translated from l'Abbé Bernard Nodet, *Le Sacerdoce, c'est l'amour du Coeur de Jésus* in *Le curé d'Ars. Sa pensée-Son Coeur* (ed. Xavier Mappus, Foi Vivante, 1966), page 189.

There are two kinds of strict obligation that apply after confession: that is, the duty to preserve the seal of confession, and the duty to correct any possible errors.

The Duty to Correct our Errors in Hearing Confessions

Concerning the second obligation, if the error or defect has to do with the validity of the sacrament (for example, omitting the words of absolution), the priest is obliged to correct it. This obligation depends on the gravity of the effect on the penitent: for instance if he had committed a grave sin, or lacked sufficient contrition, the priest should remedy the situation in the following confession. If the defect concerned the integrity of the confession, and the priest did not ask what was necessary, he should make it up in the next confession, not outside of it. If the priest actually gave erroneous advice, for instance saying that something was not a serious sin when it truly was—he should repair the damage even outside of confession, asking the penitent for permission to speak about this topic. If the confessor omitted to inform the penitent of some obligations that he had—such as to make restitution, or to flee from the occasion of sin—he should bring it up in the next confession. If the confessor actually misled the penitent by saying that he need not make restitution when he was obliged to do so, then he himself would be obliged to make restitution, unless he is able to rectify the situation in the next confession.

But what of defects in confession when there is no opportunity to see the penitent again? This can happen often in large penance services, or confessions in a public Church where the priest does not know the penitent, and there is no opportunity to see him or her again. In such cases, when the priest realizes that he did not ask the proper questions for the integrity of the confession, or gave some erroneous advice, or perhaps, cannot recall if he gave absolution properly—he must entrust these penitents to the Most Sacred Heart of Christ, and he can do some penance or private prayers afterwards asking for Christ's mercy both for himself and the penitent.

It may also happen that the confessor is quite tired or not fully alert in hearing confessions. In this case, if he suspects that a grave sin has been confessed, and he has not heard it, he should ask the penitent to repeat it, perhaps apologizing first to him or her for having been distracted. Occasionally he could ask the penitent to repeat something he didn't hear, but this should be done rarely, so as not to make the sacrament odious. He can always be sure that Christ the Good Shepherd, who is the One who truly hears everything and forgives, will make up for his deficiencies. Also the Church in her access to Christ's infinite treasures of mercy and forgiveness, makes up for the defects of her ministers. This principle is called "*Ecclesia suplet.*" But obviously the priest confessor should not presume on Christ's mercy for his own defects. He should be sufficiently alert in hearing confessions, perhaps by taking a nap beforehand, or having a cup of coffee before hearing confessions if he is sleepy. Prayers, such as the prayer to the Trinity and to the Saints, are particularly helpful in preparing the priest to give the most to his penitents, and to Christ himself, whom he is serving in the Sacrament.

The Seal of Confession

Concerning the **seal of confession**, there is a most strict obligation to keep absolutely secret anything that the penitent reveals *in ordine ad absolutionem sacramentalem* (for the purpose of obtaining sacramental absolution), and whose revelation would make the sacrament burdensome or odious (see *Code of Canon Law* (1983) [*CIC*], 983 and 984; [*CIC*], 1467). The seal includes all mortal and venial sins, and other things that if known could harm the sacrament or penitent, such as the circumstances of the sin, accomplices, defects of the penitent, etc. And all of this would apply even if absolution were not given, as long as they were revealed to the confessor in *ordine ad absolutionem sacramentalem.*

The obligation to protect the seal binds very strictly both by natural law and by divine positive and ecclesiastical law.

The violation of the seal is direct if the confessor speaks of the sin itself and the person who did it. Violation of the seal is always a grave sin, and when it is fully culpable, it carries with it the penalty of excommunication *latae sententiae* reserved to the Holy See (cf. *CIC* 1388). An indirect violation of the seal occurs if a confessor's words are close to revealing the sin of a penitent, or to making the sacrament odious. Not all indirect violations are grave sins, but they can be punished by the proper Church authority according to the gravity of the situation.

In general the good confessor must be very reserved and delicate in his speech. If possible he should say nothing about the confessions that he hears, even if there is no danger of violating the seal. It would not be appropriate for instance to mention that a certain person went to confession with him, or even that a person came to confession to him after many years—though there is no way that that person could be known. In preaching it is not good for the priest to cite confessions as the source of his knowledge or experience. The best thing is that the confessor give thanks to God for the graces that He gives to others through his ministry, and thus silently learn how to be a better and more effective instrument of God's justice and mercy as the years go by.

If the priest needs guidance on how to deal with certain sins that he has heard in confession, he may speak of these situations to an experienced and discreet priest, but only in a general, hypothetical way, and without any possibility of revealing a specific person or situation to the other priest. For instance, he might phrase his question thus to the other priest: "What advice would you give to a person in such and such circumstances?" or "How do you help people in confession who have such and such faults?"

Abuses of Confession

The priest should never ask either directly or indirectly the name of the accomplice in a sin confessed to him; this would be a grave sin in itself. In principle the penitent himself should not give the name of his accomplice. If we discover the name of the accomplice indirectly—by the questions we need to ask, or by a penitent's remarks—we should not worry, but we can make no use of his knowledge in any way.

The *Code of Canon Law* establishes that *outside of the danger of death, the absolution of an accomplice in a sin against the sixth commandment of the Decalogue is invalid* (*CIC* 977). Therefore, outside of the danger of death, to attempt to absolve an accomplice in a sin of lust would be a very grave sin. The absolution would be invalid, and the priest would incur the censure of excommunication *latae sententiae* reserved to the Holy See (cf. *CIC* 1378). The solicitation *ad turpia* is particularly serious because the priest takes advantage of his role as confessor, either directly or indirectly, within the sacrament or within the confessional, in order to seduce another to commit a sin of impurity. In the most grave cases such an action can even lead to dismissal from the clerical state (cf. *CIC* 1387).

A person who falsely denounces a priest for a solicitation *ad turpia* must make a formal retraction of his false denouncement. He may not be absolved until he does this, and until he is ready to make reparation for the damage that he has caused (cf. *CIC* 982). If a person denounces a priest falsely before an ecclesiastical Superior, he automatically falls into interdict *latae sententiae* (automatically), and if he is a cleric, he also incurs suspension.

Proper Place for Hearing Confessions

The place for hearing confessions of course should fit with the nature and dignity of the sacrament. Therefore the Church through her Canon Law has established that the proper place for hearing confessions is a Church or Chapel; by extension, we can assume that a room or space adjacent or connected to it is also permissible. To assure anonymity there should always be a screen between the priest and the penitent as well. Confessions should not be heard outside of the confessional, unless there is a just cause.

Obviously, in danger of death, confessions may be heard in any location.

Concerning the option of going to confession face to face, which has become widespread in recent years, the confessor can refuse this option, if he finds it inappropriate or compromising.[2] This may particularly apply to hearing confessions of women and children. By insisting on using the screen in these cases, the confessor protects both himself and the penitent from the danger of temptation, assures a more integral confession, and is able to give appropriate advice—especially for topics that are more personal or apply to the sixth commandment.

Prudence in Dealing with Women

While a priest is obviously a shepherd and a father to his people, he is still a human being with faults and weaknesses. He must be careful to keep away from any occasions of sin, or the possibility of giving scandal to others. Therefore in dealing with members of the opposite sex, *his manner should be characterized more by priestly gravity and prudence than by over-familiarity.* For instance, it is not appropriate for priests to be kissing and hugging women, or allowing themselves to receive such external signs of affection—unless of course the woman is his mother or a close relative. Certainly a priest must be positive and courteous with everyone, but he must avoid any sign of favoritism or attachment to specific persons, especially if they are women, since this could compromise both him and them.

---

[2] Cf. Decision by the Pontifical Council for the Interpretation of Legislative Texts, June 16th, 1998: confirmed by Pope John Paul II on July 7th, 1998.

In matters of the confessional it may be necessary at times for the priest to send a female penitent to another priest, for instance, if he begins to feel a certain attachment starting to grow towards her, or if he notices that she is becoming too personal with him, or perhaps too dependent on him. This should also be done if a certain issue relating to purity comes up in the confessional, and the priest does not know how to address or solve it. It is best then to refer the penitent to an older more experienced priest and confessor.

In visiting women who are bedridden or sick, it is a very good idea to have someone else in the house—a relative, in-law, or friend, for instance. An added caution is to keep the door slightly ajar in the room in which one is seeing the person; if he is hearing her confession, the other person(s) in the house should of course remain at a discreet distance, or in a nearby room.

The same caution applies to giving spiritual direction to women outside of the confessional. It is better to speak with them in an office or conference room that has a transparent window, or in a more public setting. In this way both the priest and the woman can avoid a compromising situation. In giving spiritual direction to women the conversations should be brief and to the point, without needless questions or familiarities.

None of the above practices mean that we do not care for women, or that we are avoiding them; it simply means that we recognize our condition as weak human beings prone to temptation—both ourselves and they. We love them as good priests and shepherds love all the faithful and all human beings, but with the mind and heart of Christ. It is clear from the Gospel that the Savior was always most prudent and careful in dealing with women, though he loved each one of them as much as he loved his male disciples, and gave his life for them.

Section VI

Hearing Confessions in Matters of Faith

Our moral life has its source in faith in God who reveals his love to us. Saint Paul speaks of the "obedience of faith" as our first obligation. He shows that "ignorance of God" is the principle and explanation of all moral deviations. Our duty toward God is to believe in him and bear witness to him.

—*CCC* 2087

Perhaps one of the greatest challenges that you will face in the confessional has to do with matters of faith. Loyal and believing Catholics today are a besieged group. There are many forces that attack the beliefs and convictions of the Catholic Church, and even the moral law itself. You'll need to be particularly patient yet clear with people who have these doubts—showing understanding, yet not wavering in the basic tenets of revealed truths and the natural moral law.

The first commandment states that you must love God above all things, and "not to have false gods before you." There are many false gods in people's lives today: money, career, popularity, and various pseudo-religious movements, like the New Age, which fascinate individuals by their apparently new beliefs and their catch words. To many the Catholic Church with her permanent teachings can appear to be stale or old-fashioned. Non-Catholic groups can also be very attractive for Catholics with little formation: often these communities have better preachers, they offer a greater feeling of "fellowship," and above all, they have fewer rules to follow, or dogmas in which to believe.

All of these things contribute to an environment which, if not openly hostile to the true Faith, at least undermines it. As a good priest confessor, you'll need to be aware of all these movements and alternative "faith experiences" which are as close to people as Internet Web sites. But even though there are myriad temptations against faith, this does not take away a person's responsibility. Faith is a supernatural virtue given to us at Baptism; God wants it to grow in the soul, with the help of his grace. But like any valuable gift, it can be lost through carelessness and irresponsibility.

With Persons Coming Back to the Church

One kind of penitent that you may encounter—I hope you get many of them—is a person coming back to the Church after many years. Perhaps she had joined some Mega-Church or Protestant group, because she felt particularly lonely at some point in her life, and found no help from her Catholic friends. Or perhaps she had just drifted away from her childhood faith when she married a non-Catholic man, who was a fervent evangelical and who convinced her to come to his community. Or perhaps at some point in her life she was more impressed with the preaching in another religion, or its use of the Bible.

Whatever the case, you'll have to judge, based on prudent questions, if she is truly culpable of grave sin. Of course in itself apostasy is a grave sin, since it is the deliberate rejection of the Church which a person knows to be the true Church founded by Christ. But given the immense confusion among Catholics in the last forty years, and above all, the very extended idea that "all religions are equal, and one must not be judgmental"—it is hard to say how many lapsed Catholics are apostates in the true sense of the word. Many today have not been formed, or even informed, to believe that Christ founded only one Church, with all the means of salvation, and that one must believe in that Church in order to be saved.

So getting back to the case of the woman penitent above, you must know a few key things in order to understand the state of her soul, and to give her the best advice. If she had very little training or Catholic formation in her life, or went to Catholic schools that were very weak and ambiguous in their teachings, be sure to give the benefit of the doubt to her, and be very welcoming—I would almost say, congratulatory—to her because she has chosen to come back to the truth. She has probably not committed a grave sin against the Faith, since she never really knew it. Perhaps you could refer her to a good Catholic study group, or some well-formed Catholics that you know, who can welcome and encourage her as she returns to the Church.

With Persons Having Doubts of Faith

At times you may hear the confession of a high school or college student who mentions doubts of Faith. This could even be the case if they attend well-known Catholic schools or colleges. You'll need to get a sense of his previous formation and background in the Church, which is always necessary to assess real responsibility for sins against faith. You may need to ask him if he is currently reading any anti-Catholic books or articles, and if he is doing so deliberately, or because they have been assigned to him at his school. You may want to ask him if he could pass his course without the need to read these books, and even suggest to him some good alternatives and sources that would counteract the negative material he is reading.

The main thing is to remind him of the greatness and truthfulness of Catholic teachings, and to pray for the grace of Faith if he is having doubts. If he is struggling to maintain his faith, he is not likely to be guilty of grave sin, but he needs to be realistic about the occasions that can lead him to sin, such as agnostic or atheistic teachers, or peers who laugh at the Catholic faith and lead immoral lives.

Attending Mass on Sundays and Holy Days

Related to people's faith and past training is certainly the issue of attending Mass on Sundays and Holy Days of Obligation. Many Catholics have not heard that attending Mass is a grave obligation. They may think it is an inspiring and good thing to do, but feel perfectly free to do whatever they wish on Sundays, as long as they remember

God in some way. Of course this way of thinking is contrary to the constant teaching of the Church, and most specifically, the *Catechism of the Catholic Church: The Sunday Eucharist is the foundation and confirmation of all Christian practice. For this reason the faithful are obliged to participate in the Eucharist on days of obligation, unless excused for a serious reason (for example, illness, the care of infants) or dispensed by their own pastor. Those who deliberately fail in this obligation commit a grave sin (CCC* 2181).

Ignorance about this commandment is compounded of course when people hear nothing about the Sunday obligation from the pulpit, or when many of their friends go up to receive Communion on Sunday when they have been away from Church for a long time. All of this points to invincible ignorance, or at least a big confusion in their minds about the real nature and importance of Sunday Mass.

The main point is to take advantage of their confession to explain in a few words why the Mass is necessary: that it is the commemoration of the greatest event in human history, the Resurrection of Christ; that it is an essential part of the third commandment, to sanctify the Sabbath Day; that it unites individuals and families in the one Body of Christ. Finally you should let them know that it is a grave sin to miss Mass on Sundays and Holy Days of Obligation, without a just reason. Such reasons could be sickness, travel with impossibility of finding a Church, the need to work to support one's family and finding no way to get time off on Sunday or the Saturday vigil, etc.

With People Hurt by Church Scandals

In a few confessions you may sense that certain people have been deeply hurt by recent sexual scandals involving priests and bishops. It has indeed been a cause for many to leave the Church, or at least to become deeply disillusioned. This situation has been exaggerated and dramatized continually by the anti-Catholic secularist media (some newspapers, TV, radio, Internet, etc.), with continuing revelations that certain bishops knew about the situation of these priests and did nothing about it.

You need to be very patient and supernatural with these people, and try to show them that the Church in her teachings and sacraments is holy, and that they should not reject Christ's spotless Bride because of the actions of very few of her priests, bishops, and lay people. That would be like rejecting the Sacrament of Marriage because of all the divorced and failed marriages in this country. Again, without being cynical, you should also be aware that the priest scandals gave the opportunity for some people to leave the Church because they did not like her teachings in the first place, or found them too hard to live by. Perhaps, appealing to Christian charity, you can encourage these people to pray for these priests, especially those that were accused falsely.

You could also ask them to examine their own conscience to see if they are the Catholics that they are supposed to be, and if their non-Catholic friends could be scandalized at times by their own words or actions. It is not only priests that give scandal by disobeying Church teachings.

Profanity and Cursing

Finally, you will have many penitents that accuse themselves of bad words or profanity. Many people confuse the use of bad words with cursing or profanity. In reality crude words are not sins in themselves, but simply express the anger of the people who use them—which in itself could be sinful. Sins against the second commandment include the taking of false oaths, which of itself is a grave sin because God's name is invoked to witness a lie, or a lighter use of God's name to express surprise, anger, lamentation, etc. The main principle is to teach people that the name of God and the saints is sacred, and should only be used in a reverent and respectful way, such as in prayer and religious instruction. It is a venial sin to use the name of God or Jesus on other occasions. Many people are in the habit of saying "Oh God" in the lightest of circumstances, or for dramatic effect, but this should not be done.

More serious is the sin of cursing, when a person asks God to damn or condemn something or someone. If said with sufficient deliberation and consent against some person, this is always a mortal sin. We must desire the salvation and happiness of people, not their damnation. An even graver sin against the second commandment is blasphemy, when a person rejects or makes fun of God, his Church, or her teachings, or the angels and saints. Often times people will make blasphemous comments in order to appear clever or "in the know," or perhaps they wish to pass themselves off as being superior to the pope or the Church.

Other times such comments can come from authentic hatred of the Church and her teachings. In either case, blasphemy is a grave sin and needs to be confessed humbly, with the firm purpose of amendment. A good penance for such persons would be to speak well of the Church to the very people before whom he had blasphemed, or to explain to them that he had spoken unjustly about the Church and is very sorry for what he said.

Irreverent jokes or comments about God or holy things can be either mortal or venial sins, depending upon the subject matter and the intention of the speaker. Such speech is wrong not only because it offends God, but it often weakens the faith of people.

In all these cases regarding the Faith, you need to go to the Holy Spirit to know the true state of the penitent's mind and heart, and how much ignorance or malice were involved in their sins against faith. In this way you can help people to make a truly integral confessions of their sins, as far as they are able at the moment, and to give clear, helpful advice to them.

Giving People Hope

Sometimes, when things turn out the very opposite of what we intended, we cry out spontaneously: "Lord, it's all going wrong, every single thing I'm doing!" The time has come for us to rectify our approach and say: "With you, Lord, I will make steady headway, because quia tu es Deus fortitudo mea (for you, O Lord, are my strength)."

— Saint Josemaría Escrivá, homily "The Christian's Hope,"
in *Friends of God*, no. 213. New York: Scepter Publishers, 1981

Giving people hope is arguably the most important task that we have as confessors, apart from giving Christ's absolution for sins. Many people seem to be discouraged today about the world and themselves. At times this may be caused by some kind of psychological depression, but it can also be a lack of trust in God's goodness and his promises to us—which is the essence of the theological virtue of hope. Some penitents may have a combination of both depression and distrust, and it may be hard to determine the degree of responsibility for their situation. In any case you should always bear in mind that hope is a supernatural virtue—it does not depend on human consolations or feelings—and that it is set in motion by a grace given by God. But God always respects people's freedom: some individuals can deliberately reject God's grace by preferring sadness and negativity.

The time for confession is usually quite brief for determining the deepest causes of a penitent's lack of hope. Often you may hear: "I get discouraged too easily"; "I'm negative about a lot of people and things"; "I get angry with God and don't trust him."

With such statements, you may need to ask gently for more details—is it his job, or his family, or his health that gets him down? Has there been a big tragedy in his life, and is he blaming God for it? If this is the case, try to show that he must not overreact, and that God does truly love him; in mysterious ways he can draw good from tough or even evil situations. At times, if the discouragement or despair is very deep, you may only be able to penetrate the person's heart a *little* bit. But at least you can provide some enlightenment for him or her, and give them something to think about.

Of course you must be assured that in some way they are sorry for their lack of hope, and that they are willing to struggle against it. As a penance you could perhaps ask them to pray several times, "Lord Jesus, I trust in you and your love for me," or to read a good book on hope and trust in God and his Providence. The reading of a Psalm can also be very helpful, such as Psalm 23 or 42.

Presumption and Other Sins

The opposite of despair is presumption. I think it is more extended in the modern world than despair, but people do not recognize it in themselves. It is really a lack of sorrow for sin, along with a poor or superficial examination of conscience. Since many Catholics have not heard much preaching about sin in recent years, they may be convinced that they have very few sins, or that their faults are very light. Ultimately they're deceiving themselves, and will end up more unhappy since they don't know themselves, and haven't really gotten to the roots of their faults, such as pride, anger, or envy. Or they are convinced that since God is all-Merciful, they need not be concerned about their sins. They forget that he is also all-Just, and that there needs to be atonement and reparation for every sin, either in this life or the next.

You may have to bring up some of these points to stir up sorrow for the sin of presumption. Perhaps you could emphasize something that the penitent knows is wrong—such as polluting the environment, or cheating on one's taxes—and then compare these to other sins. Sins against purity pollute the body and soul, for instance, or missing Mass on Sunday is to cheat God and the Church. Try to help them not to presume on God's mercy or goodness, but to make a brave and true examination of conscience, and to have a real purpose of amendment. You may not obtain 100% results in this attempt, but at least you can point the person in the right direction, for his or her good.

At times you will find people who are quite "down on themselves," and you can tell that they tend to blame themselves for many things. Try to help them to be more objective, and not to think of themselves too much. At the root of a lot of self-blaming can be a sense of inferiority, or even a hidden anger at people or situations.

Some people are very affected by what they read in the media, either of the liberal or conservative varieties. Many Web sites and blogs can promote an unrealistic and pessimistic view of the country, the economy, and even the Church. Some people may even accuse themselves of being addicted to certain Web sites and blogs, to which they're attracted, but which they know can also be a source of anger. Try to convince these people that it is wrong to give in to a lack of hope, or a pessimistic view of history, despite all the things they may be reading or hearing about. Encourage them to pray more often, trusting in Christ's Most Sacred Heart, and recalling the Apostle's magnificent words: **"For those who love God, all things work for the good"** (Rom 8:28).

As a practical point for advice, or even as a penance, you could ask them to stop looking at those media sites or sources which are the cause of their sadness or anxiety.

Sins against Charity

Of course the greatest commandment of all is to love God above all things, as mentioned before. We are not to have idols or false gods before us. With the exception of the religious or those who have a special dedication, most people will not accuse themselves of lack of love for God—though they may accuse themselves of taking his Name in vain, missing Mass on Sundays, or entertaining doubts about the Church and her teachings. It is helpful to remind them that the greatest commandment is to love God above all things, and that all the other commandments flow from this one. You can also help them to see that excessive attachment to career, physical fitness, or popularity are also forms of idol worship, including self-worship.

Most frequently people will mention that they have lacked charity with others. This could include impatience or yelling, rude remarks, being short in their comments, holding grudges, and gossiping. Perhaps a good way to help these people is to show that anger often comes from stress or pent-up emotions. They need to trust in God more and his goodness, and perhaps, even to relax and exercise more. In this way they will be more understanding and fair-minded with others. You could also give them a bit of advice on how to handle unwanted situations like extra work, long traffic jams (this can be an excellent way to make atonement for sins, and to offer sacrifice for the souls in Purgatory), or annoying personalities at home or at work.

Rather than becoming angry at these situations, which is useless anyway, teach them to connect them with the Cross of Christ. Pope Benedict XVI in his encyclical *Spe Salvi* speaks of the value of *offering up things*, a term used commonly before by many Catholics and which can have great supernatural meaning: *Those who did so* (offer things up) *were convinced that they could insert these little annoyances into Christ's great "compassion" so that they somehow become part of the treasury of compassion so greatly needed by the human race. In this way, even the small inconveniences of daily life could acquire meaning and contribute to the economy of good and of human love* (no. 40).

Concerning others, you could also ask if they have apologized to the person they have offended, either in word or deed—and if they have sincerely forgiven those who have offended them.

Omissions and Obligations

When helping people to make integral confessions, you should also ask if they are aware of any *omissions* in charity. That is, was there a time when they should have helped someone in need? And out of indifference or laziness, did they neglect to do so? The person in need could be an individual at work, a neighbor, and more often, a family member. In extraordinary cases, it could be a person in prison, or a woman who is thinking of having an abortion. Charity is the most beautiful of the virtues since it consists in imitating Christ by doing good for others—but often people are nearsighted and think only of their own immediate needs or problems. You might remind your penitents from time to time of Christ's powerful words: **"As long as**

you did it for one of these, the least of my brothers, you did it for me" (Mt 25:40).

At times people will have a definite *obligation* of charity—towards a parent, a co-worker, a friend. In a general way all of us have the obligation to help innocent people whose lives or welfare are threatened: I would say that as a nation, all of us particularly have the obligation to help unborn children, who have been almost totally deprived of their right to life. We must all do our part to help them, through our words and actions, and particularly in the way we vote in elections. If we know of a grave threat to the body or soul of an individual, and we do nothing, we are guilty of a grave sin against charity, and possibly justice as well.

Charity of course means not only giving money or material help to persons in need, but also assisting him or her to find God, and in many cases, to return to the Church and the sacraments. Perhaps you could encourage a penitent who has a friend that has been away from the Church to pray particularly for him and offer some sacrifice; then maybe he could give a good book to him, or have a deeper conversation with him or her. **"There will be more joy in heaven over one sinner who repents, than over ninety-nine who had no need or repentance."** (Lk 15:7) And on another occasion Christ stated, **"He who gives witness to me before men, I will give witness to him before my father in Heaven."** (Mt 10:32) We have the obligation to speak up if the Church and her teachings are being attacked, or the moral law is being denied. By being silent, we allow error and falsehood to be propagated. In other words, often times both charity and justice will demand that good Catholics give personal and public witness to their Faith.

Gossip or Tale-bearing

Another area of faults against charity is tale-bearing or gossip. Many people, both men and women, accuse themselves of this. It is one of the most common sins. Yet many are confused about it at the same time, and could mistake some type of speech with gossip. Is it wrong, for instance, for a man to "vent" to his wife about the unjust demands that his boss is making of him at work? Or for a woman to mention how humiliated and insulted she felt at a neighbor's remark to her? The moral principle about charity in speech states that we may not discuss the faults of others unless we have sufficient cause. Sufficient cause could be the need to get good advice or consolation about a hard situation that is truly bothering us, or the desire to help others and therefore the need to discuss another's fault with someone who can give good advice to us, or at least pray with us for a solution. At other times we may need to warn others of a person's faults, which could be a physical or spiritual danger to them—such as a man who distributes pornography, or a woman who promotes contraception, or even a priest who says confusing and misleading things from the pulpit.

In effect, the sin of gossip is to reveal others' faults for vain or selfish motives: to while away time, to get revenge on somebody, to appear superior to others, to laugh or make fun of somebody. Rash judgment is related to gossip, for in this case a person judges another to have committed a sin or to be at fault in some area without sufficient evidence. And even if a person has objectively committed a sin, we have no right to reveal that fault without sufficient reason, as we said above.

Many people will say that it is very hard to avoid gossip, since everyone is doing it at work or in social settings, and they do not want to appear strange or isolated by their silence. The old refrain "silence is golden" may have relevance here for a penitent, or maybe you could suggest that with a little creativity he or she could change the direction of uncharitable conversations by asking the group a few questions, such as: "Can we do anything to help this person out of this situation? What good does it do to keep complaining about this; doesn't it just lower our own morale?" Or one may even be able to say: "Looks like there's nothing we can do. Let's at least pray for this person." The main point is that a good Christian should not contribute to uncharitable conversations, but should try to change their direction.

Section VII

The Need for Justice

The seventh commandment forbids unjustly taking or keeping the goods of one's neighbor and wronging him in any way with respect to his goods. It commands justice and charity in the care of earthly goods and the fruits of men's labor. For the sake of the common good, it requires respect for the universal destination of goods and respect for the right to private property.

— *CCC* 2401

Justice is that virtue by which we give each person his or her due. It is applicable throughout our life: in the family, in school, in business, in any social context. You may hear from boys and girls who accuse themselves of "cheating" in school or in games. Usually these will be venial sins, but it could be helpful to ask what kind of cheating was involved—was it taking a few answers on a quiz from a friend, or was it plagiarizing an entire term paper? Others may be guilty of theft or destruction of property, and you will need to ask how much was taken, and how much damage was done—always remembering the requirement to make restitution in order to show true sorrow.

More complex and serious are lapses of adults in matters of justice. This could range from stealing computer software to embezzling millions of dollars, or to cheating clients and stockholders. Some penitents prefer to be very general about these sins, or try to downplay them—but again, as a good priest confessor, you must help people to make an *integral confession* as best they can, here and now. Confession is the moment of truth, not only before you, but before God. It is necessary to confess grave sins in number and specific kind. So if a person says that he charged a client too much—be sure to find out how much he was overcharged, and what harm was done to the client. If it involved tax evasion, be sure to ask how much was involved. It might be worthwhile to speak with a good Catholic businessman about marketing and sales techniques, along with profit margins, so that you are not ignorant about what businessmen face today—and what practices are considered to be ethical or unethical.

At the same time, recall that for every sin against justice there is an obligation to make restitution, as said before. If this can be done immediately, all the better. But if the person is not in a position to do this, he must try to do it gradually until the full debt is paid back. He does not have to turn himself in, or reveal himself as the thief—but he is obliged to make restitution, even if secretly. This is called "occult compensation." For instance, if he has cheated a company for the amount of $1,000, he should provide $1,000 worth of services for free—either by working extra hours without pay, or in some other manner. It is usually sufficient for the penitent to promise the priest to make restitution, in order to receive absolution. The priest need not ask all the specific steps he will use to make restitution, though he could give him some ideas. The main point is that he is assured of his purpose of amendment.

Raising People's Sights

Usually people will not accuse themselves of a lack of "social justice." Normally it will be in terms of smaller things like not paying bills on time, cheating in class, not giving correct information on insurance claims, overcharging on expense accounts, or taking more than the correct change in supermarkets. But in giving good advice to people, try to raise their sights to the greater community around them. They cannot lead isolated lives, and one act of injustice eventually hurts the entire community.

As citizens of a country, we are obligated to contribute to the common good as best we can: to achieve proper housing and nutrition for all, to assure an adequate education, to protect innocent human lives, to provide proper health care and job opportunities.

While we all have duties towards others, be particularly aware of those who are in a position to help others more: single people, who have extra time and money on their hands; retired people in good health who have the ability to volunteer their time; wealthy individuals who have more than enough to support themselves and their families, and can truly help others with their "time, talent, and treasure." Rather than spending all kinds of time and money on jewelry, travel and luxury vacation trips—encourage them to contribute funds to a soup kitchen in a poor neighborhood, or to an inner-city training or educational program. To those who are self-absorbed it is good to recall the parable of Lazarus and the rich man (cf. Lk 16:19–31); they should examine their consciences about what they are doing with the material means that God has given to them.

The Question of Tithing

Some Catholics may ask about the duty of tithing. This is a highly recommendable practice, and you can encourage people to give even more than ten percent of their income if they are able, without detriment to their families. Tithing is most properly given to the things of God, namely the Church and her needs—such as parish expenses, the support of Catholic seminaries, the Missions, Catholic Charities, and the apostolates of good Catholic institutions which are serving people in different ways throughout the world. You can tell these people, even *assure* them, that God does not let himself be outdone in generosity. Families that unstintingly and regularly give their means to him and others will not be left destitute. As he sent the manna in the desert to the people of Israel, he also provides for those who are generous with him and his Church.

An exception to the tithing practice certainly could be made to those in severe economic straits, or to those just beginning a family. In such cases be sure to encourage them to be generous also; it is always praiseworthy to take a certain financial "risk" for God, even though they may not be able to give a full ten percent of their income right away.

Family Duties

In creating man and woman, God instituted the human family and endowed it with its fundamental constitution. Its members are persons equal in dignity. For the common good of its members and society, the family necessarily has manifold responsibilities, rights, and duties.

— CCC 2203

The command to honor one's parents has deep connections with the virtue of gratitude. A child should be grateful to his parents for all that he has received from them, and should therefore respect and obey them in all that is just. Though adults can also disobey, of course, it is children who most accuse themselves of disrespect or disobedience. In hearing their confessions, try to explain in simple terms that they should obey not simply to avoid punishment, or to receive favors from their parents—but out of gratitude for the gift of life, and for the support and love that they have received from them. They mustn't be little egotists, thinking only of their fun or entertainment. They should be prompt in obeying their parents, and even, as they grow older, they can volunteer to do things before they're asked. In this way they will make their home a happier and better place to live, and give good example to their siblings.

You may also have to remind adult men and women at times about proper care for their own parents. Though they are not bound by obedience to them any more, they will always be bound by justice and gratitude. They should make sure that their parents are well cared for in their old age or in sickness, that they are not abandoned or neglected. It is very sad to see large numbers of elderly persons in retirement facilities, or perhaps living alone, who are not visited by their children or grandchildren. This can be a grave sin against the fourth commandment, especially if the parents' need is great and there is deliberate neglect of basic care and affection for them.

Honoring One's Children

But we can also say that the fourth commandment asks parents to "honor their children." First they should receive them gratefully: beginning in the womb they should not be considered as burdens, but as gifts from God. Each boy or girl is made in the image of God, and is entitled to his parents' love and care from the moment of conception. They also have the right to be nurtured and educated properly. As the children grow older, a common fault among couples is to be either too harsh or too permissive. Either one eventually harms the child. Harshness can crush their spirits, or make them defiant; permissiveness can make them soft and overly demanding.

At times you may be able to give some human advice about encouraging and disciplining children, based on your own experiences and your dealing with families, but you must always remember that each family is different, with different needs and circumstances. You might ask dads if they spend sufficient time with their children, if they discuss each child's development regularly with their wives, if they pray for them each day. Mothers often need to be more patient with their children, knowing how to say things with kind and encouraging words, rather than resorting to yelling or threats. But we priests must also have a lot of understanding for their situation. With many small children to care for, and no one to help her during the day, a mother can feel quite burdened and tired. Nevertheless with prayer, proper rest, and perhaps some timely conversations with other mothers, they can find good support and balance.

Upon occasion it's helpful to remind mothers that theirs is the most important work in the world: there is no substitute for making a home, and raising children with love and care. Often they can be made to feel inferior by the influence of the world, the lifestyles of other women, or by radical feminist ideas which downplay a mother's role in the home. As a compassionate and understanding priest confessor, you can do a lot to encourage these women in their work at home, which is often heroic since they receive no recognition nor thanks for what they are doing.

Most importantly, parents have the duty of forming their children humanly and spiritually. They have this duty from the natural moral law itself, which cannot be transferred to others except in a secondary way. They must assure that their children develop basic human virtues, or good habits of thinking and acting that will perfect them as human beings and prepare them to be of service to others in society. Such basic virtues include truthfulness, work, responsibility, charity, chastity, and generosity. They also have the obligation to give their children basic religious training. Certainly good schools and outside programs can assist them, but their children's essential attitude towards God and the Church, their moral conduct and way of praying, must come from the home. It is important that the family pray together, such as at meals and at bedtime. Recommend that the family go to Holy Mass together as often as possible, since Christ in the Holy Eucharist strengthens and unites the members of a family in his divine love and providence.

Parents should also be particularly vigilant these days with use of the Internet by their children. Unfortunately cyberspace has become a jungle of danger and temptation for many individuals. Indecent pictures, immoral stories and conversations, even direct solicitation to sin are quite common. Parents should not assume that their young teens will be able to resist the immense pressure from the outside to look at these things, and to give in to them. As a precaution, both Dad and Mom need to work together to protect their children; at times this could mean the installation of a strong filtering system at home, placing the computer in a public place, and monitoring use of emails and other cyber-communications. You can tell parents that they should not be naïve in this matter. While avoiding an attitude of distrust towards their children, or a constant suspicion of them, they cannot take things for granted either.

Sins against the Fifth Commandment

> *Human life is sacred because from its beginning it involves the creative action of God and it remains forever in a special relationship with the Creator, who is its sole end. God alone is the Lord of life from its beginning until its end: no one can under any circumstance claim for himself the right directly to destroy an innocent human being.*

> —CCC 2258

Respect or disrespect towards human life is a major issue in the world today—and in people's personal lives and experiences. Apart from grave sins such as procured abortion, euthanasia, and drug abuse, there is a multitude of ways in which people can harm themselves and others, both physically and morally.

One is the abuse of food and drink. Oftentimes it is not simply the disordered attachment to the pleasure of eating and drinking. Many individuals abuse food and alcohol because they feel unstable or are running from something. It is often a means of escape from loneliness and frustration, or it is a lack of purpose or hope in their lives. We priests should know this, without the need to become psychologists or therapists. By a discreet question or observation within confession, you may be able to open a world of hope for a person suffering from habitual gluttony or drunkenness, and begin his or her liberation. With the help of God's grace, we must encourage penitents to overcome that disorder which not only hurts their bodies, but their minds and souls. To receive a penance of fasting for a couple of days, or abstaining from alcohol for a period of time can be very helpful for these people. God will give them the grace to overcome their vices.

At times it may be necessary to recommend a psychologist or a professional program, if the addiction is strong. But prayer and spiritual advice should never be lacking in the person's struggle, since they also form part of the solution.

Often, especially among men, you will find the disorder of over-working. Though it is easy to assert that one must work very hard in "today's world" to support a family, one can also use work as a means of escape from family responsibilities, and even from God. A man (or woman) who doesn't pray, who is often away from the family, or who only thinks of professional work, needs to change his or her behavior. Perhaps he can begin with little things, but which are also big things, like coming home in time for supper always, and going out with one's wife at least once a week.

With some penitents you may want to ask if they take care of their health. This is also part of the fifth commandment. People should get enough sleep, they should eat properly, and they should exercise. All of these things are not luxuries, but part of God's loving plan for them, and for their families. Lack of proper sleep and exercise can produce irritability, lack of alertness, and poor work habits. They can also lead to serious health problems.

Occasionally you will meet an individual, usually single, who has the opposite problem. Physical fitness and eating habits have become idols in his or her life. With these people you should encourage generosity and care for others. Rather than use all their free time for personal exercise or body building, perhaps they could volunteer to help in a good sports or fitness program that will benefit the community. Or they could train for a marathon that will benefit handicapped children.

At times you may simply have to give common sense advice. If someone has a contagious disease, they should separate themselves from others as much as possible, or stay at home from work. If they have a cold—as many people can get during the winter time—they should alert people around them if they are at work, avoiding the shaking of people's hands, washing their hands frequently, and carrying a handkerchief so that they do not cough or sneeze towards others. These are not scrupulous measures, but deeds of charity towards the health of others.

The Sin of Scandal

Apart from harming others physically, some people forget or gloss over the *moral* harm that they can do to others, and fail to make reparation for it. *Scandal is an attitude or behavior which leads another to do evil. The person who gives scandal becomes his neighbor's tempter. He damages virtue and integrity; he may even draw his brother into spiritual death* (*CCC* 2284). For instance, a man who misses Mass on Sunday without a good reason gives bad example to his wife and children. A woman who neglects her duties at home gives bad example to her husband and children. The older brother who watches a bad movie can be leading his younger brothers and sisters into sin. A man who constantly criticizes others and gossips at work is leading others into the sin of detraction, or even slander.

For these reasons, the good priest confessor should ask the circumstances surrounding some sins. If a man uses bad language, were there others present? If a woman has doubts of faith, did she keep these to herself, or did she voice her doubts to others? The point is that a person who leads another into sin commits the sin of scandal, and has the obligation to make reparation for his words or actions. The sin could be either mortal or venial, depending on the harm that was done, and the knowledge and willfulness of the person committing the scandal.

As a good confessor, you have the obligation to ask the penitent to make reparation or atonement for any scandal he has caused. For instance, if a person has spoken badly of another, he should try to speak well of him on another occasion, or at least to tell others that his words about that person were not helpful or appropriate. If he has actually lied about someone's behavior, he is obliged to correct his error. The obligation to make reparation, of course, applies to those who provide false or misleading information in newspapers or other forms of communication, or to men or women who physically expose themselves in an immoral way for entertainment or money. There is a need to make up for the scandal committed by these acts, and the harm done to others. Similarly if a person has shown his friends indecent pictures on the Internet, he should get rid of the bad links on his computer right away, apologize to his friends, and even recommend a good filter to his friends to block such sites.

In all of these ways, the good priest confessor is not only a minister of God's mercy, but also of his Justice. God's Justice demands that there should be reparation and atonement for sins against himself and others. If a person is not willing to make up for the scandal that he or she has caused, or at least attempt to do so—he should not receive absolution.

Section VIII

The Indispensable Virtue
of Chastity

The chaste person maintains the integrity of the powers of life and love placed in him. This integrity ensures the unity of the person; it is opposed to any behavior that would impair it. It tolerates neither a double life nor duplicity in speech.

— *CCC* 2338

As we all know, this virtue has been derided, misunderstood, and deformed by many in the modern (or post-modern) world. As a result there is much confusion about human sexuality, the nature of a man and woman, the relationship between sex and having children, matters of entertainment, etc. While a priest may feel overwhelmed by the enormity of the moral challenges in this area, he cannot give up trying to form people's consciences, and helping them to make sincere and integral confessions. He must rely always on the grace of God, which enters even the most hidden crevices of people's souls, and transforms them. If he himself is living his celibate vocation well, that is, if he avoids occasions of sin, if he keeps busy in his priestly work, if he has a strong devotion to the Body of Christ in the Eucharist, and has frequent recourse to Mary, his own priesthood will be much stronger, and he will be able to help many men and women to struggle courageously and to live chastity better in their lives.

It is also very helpful for him to know some of the central insights of Pope John Paul II's *Theology of the Body* (or good popularized versions of it) which has helped many people, particularly of the younger generation, to appreciate the nature of their sexuality, and to see Matrimony as the culmination of the gift of self, both in a physical and affective way.

Chastity is truly an affirmation of love, as Saint Josemaría Escrivá, the founder of Opus Dei, often taught. Even in its prohibitions purity is an affirmation of love in a clean and complete way—both for God, and for a couple within Matrimony. It also allows a person to see himself and others more clearly and positively, and to pray with greater effectiveness. In the words of Christ himself: **"Blessed are the pure of heart, for they shall see God."** (Mt 5:8)

Part of growing in this virtue is to have the courage and humility to admit one's faults and weaknesses, and to seek forgiveness for sins. It is easy to justify all kinds of sins in this area, especially with intellectual and psychological reasonings, or with superficial slogans such as "Everyone is doing it," or "This is the twenty-first century, let's not be old-fashioned."

The truth is that chastity is a virtue absolutely necessary for salvation, and even for being a good human being. *All Christ's faithful are called to lead a chaste life in keeping with their particular states of life. At the moment of his Baptism, the Christian is pledged to lead his affective life in chastity* (CCC 2348). Therefore the priest in hearing confessions should be attentive to helping men and women make sincere and integral confessions in this area, to instructing and forming them as much as possible, and to encouraging them with specific and sound advice. In this way the sacrament of forgiveness will truly be the sacrament of grace and renewal that it is meant to be.

Assuring Integral Confessions in Matters of Chastity

In order to fulfill your role as judge and shepherd, you need to assure the formal integrity of a confession—as said before; that is, that the penitent should say all unconfessed grave sins that he is able to confess at that moment. In matters relating to purity, this could be more difficult for people, given the delicate nature of the subject and the possibility of shame. Many times, therefore, you will have to ask a few questions to assure this integrity, especially because of the laxity and ignorance of many people in matters of chastity, and their inability to examine their consciences well.

At the same time you need to be delicate and careful in your way of asking, considering what the penitent here and now needs to say, given his or her condition of soul. You should not only ask about sins against chastity, but other areas as well, since there are many other matters where people have become lax, or their consciences have been deformed, such as attendance at Sunday Mass, professional or family duties, omissions in charity, etc. If you only ask a penitent about the sixth commandment, you could give the impression that you are obsessed with the matter, or have an unwholesome curiosity.

When we do need to identify a specific sin against chastity, with its pertinent circumstances, we must ask what is necessary to discover the real dispositions and conditions of the penitent's soul, which often includes causes of the sin, occasions, and possible obligations of reparation (for engendering a child out of wedlock, for instance). Especially in dealing with young people we should not ask about sins that they do not know about, though we must also realize that sexual sins are now more widespread than before, and that even pre-teenage boys and girls may know things or have done things that were not known or done by an older generation.

Contraception vs. True Married Love

For married people, we need to be aware of the entire issue of openness to children. Because contraception is so widespread, and there is great ignorance as well as dissent by many Catholics on this issue, we must be both prudent and courageous in our questions. If a person has not been to confession in a long time, or has had poor formation in the Catholic faith, we should ask him if he is open to new life in his marriage. At times we will have to give a brief explanation beforehand of the greatness of married love, which includes fidelity to and support for the other spouse, as well as openness to new life. If in bringing up this topic we discover that a person has a truly invincible ignorance, and/or does not have the capacity to change his or her contraceptive behavior at that moment, we need not confront the person directly about it, since we may push the person into formal sin. At the same time, according to the *Vademecum* issued by the Pontifical Council of the Family (1997), we do have the duty to instruct and encourage the person to accept and live the truth of marital relations. We cannot allow the "law of pastoral gradualness" to become the "gradualness of the law" (cf. *Vademecum*, 3.9–10). Perhaps we can give the person something to read on the Church's teachings, ask him or her to think and pray about it, and then to come back the next time to continue speaking about it.

At times we will have to challenge an individual firmly to change his or her behavior, if it is objectively wrong. If we discover that the person is using an abortofacient pill, we should make the person aware of the evil being done, even at the risk of a negative reaction. The reason for this is that such a pill presents a real danger that an innocent human life may be destroyed. This is a proportionately serious reason for us to inform the person clearly about the evil being done. We should also be aware that all the pills on the market that are simply called contraceptives are also often abortofacient.

If a couple is using natural family planning to avoid children, we should realize that this decision is up to the couple to make, but that there should be a serious or just reason behind it, since they are limiting both the unitive and procreative capacity of their married love. If it appears that there is not a just reason, or that the previous reason no longer applies, we could suggest that the person rethink or pray about his or her decision, since God is desirous always to create human souls and to bring new life to the world.

We should also be prepared to hear from persons who have been sterilized, and be able to give some appropriate counsel for their situation, especially taking into account the person's age, disposition, and the medical possibility of reversing the sterilization.

General Observations and Some Specific Cases

In questions and answers regarding purity, both priest and penitent should avoid detailed or graphic descriptions, given the delicate nature of the matter. Generally, it is better to **say less than more** because of the danger of giving scandal or of causing temptation. If the penitent begins giving unnecessary or graphic details, then the priest should terminate the conversation in a gentle but firm way. He only needs to know what is necessary for an integral confession, though at times he may not be able to obtain it given the nature of the topic, and the need to avoid making the sacrament odious. He should not be concerned if during a confession he experiences some physical reaction to what he hears, as long as he does not consent to it, and simply lets it pass. His purpose is to be a physician of souls, but he is also a man of flesh and blood; he need not worry if his feelings or body react at times in certain ways, as long as he is trying to act with rectitude and prudence, and to help the penitent to make a sincere confession.

With **scrupulous** people who may think that a mere temptation or thought against purity is a grave sin, or who may consider their involuntary imaginings to be a mortal sin (when they are not), we must be understanding and patient. We can tell them, for instance, that unless they had full knowledge and gave complete consent to a thought or an action, they could not have committed a grave sin. They should not go over things again and again in their minds to be absolutely sure of their state of soul. This can be a stratagem of the devil to complicate them, or make them give up. Above all, scrupulous people should completely obey their confessor's instruction, and not keep doubting or turning things over in their minds. In some cases, we may have to forbid them from coming to confession for a while, so that they can see things more objectively. In serious cases they may need to be referred for good professional help.

More current today, however, are people with **lax** consciences. Given the environment of casual sex and promiscuity, and the fact that many couples are living together before marriage, many penitents may not even think that fornication or other impure actions are sins—especially if their good friends are doing it, and they have never heard any instruction about it from the pulpit or in their schools. In this case we will need to instruct them clearly and perhaps say strong and direct things like "sex before marriage is a grave sin," or "masturbation is a serious fault." It may be that certain people have invincible ignorance about the most basic things; in which case, you the priest, like a compassionate shepherd and physician, must instruct them and encourage them to live chastely, with the help of God's grace. Ignorance is not bliss when it comes to grave sins that do damage to individuals and families.

As we mentioned in a previous chapter, if a person reveals a mortal sin against purity committed some time before and not confessed because of shame, he should make a general confession, since none of his subsequently confessed mortal sins have been absolved, and his sacramental confessions have been invalid. When he has sincerely accused himself of all mortal sins committed since the first unconfessed one—including any bad confessions and unworthy communions—he should feel at peace. But this should not justify future laxity in his examination of conscience. It could be helpful to tell the person that he may discover other sins than the ones that he has just confessed, and if they are grave and not confessed, he should confess them in his next confession, without the need to repeat all the others that he has confessed already.

At times it may be hard for the penitent and confessor to determine the reason for not confessing a previous sin against purity. Part of the reason could be shame, part of it could be ignorance or doubt about the sin itself at that time, part of it could be a lack of formation about the need to make an integral confession of sins because the person was never told that it was necessary. In these cases, if there is not moral certainty that the person deliberately hid a sin that he knew was grave, he need not make a general confession or answer questions about a subject that has no clear answer. But he should confess the sin clearly at that point.

At times, on retreats or other occasions, people may recall sins of their past life, for which they are very ashamed, and not remember if they have confessed them or not, since they occurred long ago. In these cases, if the person has made a general confession before, or has been a faithful Catholic all of his life and has gone to confession regularly, he should not worry further about it and put it in God's hands. If however, out of sorrow and atonement, he would like to repeat a certain sin in confession, he may certainly do so.

Helping the Penitent to Be Sincere and Specific

In hearing confessions—not only for those relating to the sixth commandment—it is usually preferable to let the penitent speak all that is in his mind and heart first, and then ask any necessary questions or observations based on what he says, for the sake of completeness. Unless there is manifest insincerity, most penitents are agreeable and even grateful for this opportunity; since they have taken the trouble to come to confession to have their sins forgiven, and desire a true reconciliation with God; they may even suspect that their preparation for confession has not been as thorough as it should have been.

In matters of purity, however, the priest should be particularly brief yet clear in his questions, to help the person be sincere and specific. We must not allow the person simply to confess generalities, or to speak evasively. It is therefore not enough for a person to say simply "I have sinned against the sixth commandment," or "I have been impure." We will need to ask tactfully if the sin was with oneself alone, or with another; and if with another, was it with a man or a woman, and was the man or woman married. Finally, in sins against purity with another, it is usually sufficient, if the person is very reticent or not forthcoming, to ask simply if the impure action reached the point of removing clothing. This is sufficient to determine the specific sin involved, along with the number of times it was done (whether approximately, or over a certain time period).

Thoughts and Desires

Concerning thoughts and desires against purity, you should help the person distinguish between feeling and consenting. Many thoughts or desires can come to a person's mind that are wrong, but at that stage they are only temptations. The sin consists in deliberately fostering or dwelling on such thoughts and desires. As long as the person is struggling against them, even if they keep coming back, there will not be grave sin, though there may be venial sin if he does not get rid of them as firmly and quickly as he should. If there is real consent to the thoughts, the person need not describe what they were, but only give the number of times that he consented, at least approximately. If he consented to impure desires, however, he should say specifically what he desired—adultery, fornication, etc.— since sin takes place when the will deliberately desires to carry out an action that is wrong.

Helping People to Be Sincere

The questions that you ask should help the penitent to know himself better, and therefore should be asked in a positive way—like a kind and understanding physician examining a patient—so that the person feels at peace, while revealing the nature of his fault. You must avoid any kind of question that could lead to insincerity, making it difficult for the penitent to confess some sin. In certain sins against chastity, if the person is hesitant or unable to give the number of times, it may help to ask him if it was a very high number of times, so that he does not feel so guilty: "Did you commit this sin fifty times a day?" for instance. Or you could ask if the person was doing these acts over a long period of time, or a shorter period, and if they were few or many times. As you speak, be sure to avoid an accusing or bitter tone of voice, which could annoy or alienate the penitent; but also avoid speaking in too light-hearted a way, if the matter is objec-tively serious. Finally, we should not give the impression that we are naïve, for then the penitent will be insincere since he does not want to scandalize us.

At times, if a person continues to see the same priest, it might take a while before his conscience is entirely cleared, though he will always be obliged to confess any grave sins as he knows them to assure formal integrity. As time goes by, the penitent's conscience will be better formed, and he will become more sincere and refined in his confessions. We should also be aware of the signs of a penitent who is not totally sincere in his confession, especially in matters of purity: for instance, if he simply narrates his sins, or gives the impression that he is not really sorry for them; if he never speaks about chastity, or does so only in a veiled or indirect way; if he becomes nervous in the confessional, without apparent cause; if he never speaks of real sins, but only little faults or imperfections; if he shows an attitude of arrogance or criticism. Rather than treating such people harshly, realize that at least they have had enough good will to come to con-fession, and gently try to help them to be more sincere. You may not get a one hundred percent result from your efforts, but you can help them to think and pray about things, and possibly set the stage for their coming back to you.

Forming and Encouraging People

As faithful ministers of Christ, we cannot leave people in igno-rance of the basic principles of the moral law, and of the com-mandments which are necessary to obtain eternal life. We have an obligation to inform people that some actions are intrinsically wrong since they violate God's law as well as the dignity of the human per-son, such as homosexual acts, masturbation, contraception, and other impure actions. We should also form them so that they avoid the occasions of sin, know how to reject impure thoughts and desires, guard their senses, live modesty in dress and speech, and be aware of the difference between feeling something and consenting to it.

Within confession, it is very helpful to ask the Holy Spirit for the *gift of tongues*, so that we communicate the Church's teachings clearly and simply, and move people to rectify their behavior. For this reason we should be aware of certain arguments or modern considerations that will help people understand and even love what the Church teaches. Such terms as "don't cheat before marriage," "being true to one another," "leading a clean life," "respecting your girl friend," "the complete gift of self in marital relations, without barriers or calculations," can often be more effective today with people than an argument or discussion from a theology manual or moral treatise, though the basic principles of the moral law do not change.

In general the confessor should not go into details about male or female biology with penitents, much less provide explanations about the origin of human life, or the nature of the sexual act, though perhaps at some time he may have to point out briefly the practice of NFP for someone who needs to know about it. In all these matters it is better to refer the person to a competent physician or a relative of the same sex with good formation, or recommend a good book to read. The priest should limit himself to teaching the morality of sexual relations, and not get into more specific details.

Forming Young People in Schools

If you are a teacher or chaplain at a school for young persons you should make sure that the books and instructors of Religion present the teachings of the Church in a faithful and positive way, and never present sex as something merely mechanical or functional, without speaking of its morality and ultimate purpose within marriage. It is most useful that the children's parents also have exposure to the good materials that their children are receiving. You should be aware of what other teachers may be saying about sexuality to the children, especially in subjects such as Biology, Natural Science, Literature and Art, so that the students at the school are receiving a consistent and wholesome view of human sexuality, one which helps them to appreciate its beauty and purpose. Young men and women could also be told that in many ways they will have to "create a clean environment" in society by their own effort and example in this matter; they should be prepared for a difficult battle at times, but God will help them.

Some Practical Points

Both as a confessor and spiritual director of souls, be sure to remember a number of very practical points that can help everyone, younger and older, to live the virtue of chastity well: the importance of dressing and speaking modestly; guarding one's senses of sight, hearing and touch; the courage to flee from occasions of sins, such as certain persons or gatherings, along with certain movies and images on the Internet and related places; the offering of voluntary mortification and penance; frequenting the sacraments, especially sacramental confession; complete sincerity in personal spiritual direction, without hiding things out of fear or shame; good use of time which keeps the mind occupied with noble and positive things; acts of contrition and reparation for sins committed; and finally a tender devotion to Mary Mother of God, so that she can help them to lead a clean and holy life.

Try to help people see that in these matters they must speak about problems **before** rather than afterwards, to obtain both prayers and good advice. But if they happen to have a fall against purity, they must not despair, but should get up again immediately by making an act of contrition and receiving God's forgiveness in confession. In this way their fall can be converted into a victory for Jesus Christ.

Related to the struggle to live chastity, Saint Josemaría Escrivá has some excellent practical advice that also has deep scriptural roots. After speaking to the reader of the positive value of purity both for married and single people, he states that "You should also get into the habit of taking the battle to areas that are far removed from the main walls of the fortress. We cannot go about doing balancing acts on the very frontiers of evil. . . . We ought as well to fill all our time with intense and responsible work, in which we seek God's presence, because we must never forget that we have been bought at a great price and that we are temples of the Holy Spirit." (*Friends of God*, Homily "For They Shall See God." New York: Scepter Publishers, no. 186, pp. 294–295)

In general it is important to encourage people to speak sincerely about these matters; by holding them inside, like anything else, they can become exaggerated and complicated. The good priest confessor and spiritual director knows how to foster sincerity in people, without being indiscreet or rude. Some individuals may become exhausted and fearful about something they did, or something that happened to them; they simply need to speak about it to feel relief, and certainly, if there was any objective blame on their part, to confess it and then forget about it. The history of the Church is filled with examples of men and women who had serious falls in purity but then became great saints, and later accomplished tremendous good through their words and examples.

In dealing with people who are dating or with engaged couples, we should encourage them to be refined and respectful of each other's body. If they wish to show affection for one another, it should be the type of affection that they would show if their mothers were present, or someone whose character they respect. They should also be careful not to be alone with each other for any length of time if this would be an occasion of sin; since they are not married, any actions between them that deliberately arouse carnal or venereal pleasure would be grave sins. We could also let them know that, statistically, chaste relationships in dating and courting lead to the best and most lasting marriages.

Section IX

Giving Spiritual Guidance within Confession

The first and most important result of penance is reconciliation with God. This of course is the purpose of the sacrament, and the main reason that people confess their sins to us. Our words of counsel may be more or less helpful to people, but are quite secondary compared to the forgiveness of their sins; as confessors we must always remember this, lest we exaggerate our own importance. The other great effect of the sacrament, besides the forgiveness of sins, is a specific grace to improve in one's life, often accompanied by a great sense of peace and even joy. It is Christ himself, of course, who is the principal Cause of both of these graces.

But the priest confessor does have a role to play in seconding the action of Christ and his Holy Spirit. For he, too, is a physician and shepherd of souls. As his experience in the confessional increases, he will be able to perceive better the kind of penitent he has before him, and what he or she really needs to hear. A person who is rather prideful and wants to be in control obviously needs to be more humble, which perhaps means listening more to others and serving them. The good natured, easy-going kind of person may need to have more discipline and order in his life. A person who is skeptical and doubtful about himself and the world obviously needs to have more hope, and perhaps, simply needs to learn how to smile more. Like a good physician, the priest confessor develops a greater sensitivity to these personal traits as time goes by, and he can respond more effectively with on-target advice. A good part of this is the ability to recognize a predominant fault in people, and to help the penitent discover it in himself. Sometimes just a brief comment or observation within confession can open up vast horizons for people.

He is also able to detect virtues in people, and knows how to motivate them toward the good. If a person is naturally a leader and takes control of things, we can encourage him to do more for Christ and his Church, or perhaps to use his time more in the service of others, rather than for his own work or career. If a person is more thoughtful and reflective about things, she can be given good things to read or to pray about. If a person is more emotional, and leads from the heart more, as the saying goes, we can steer him towards devotions such as to the *Sacred Heart of Jesus* or to specific saints, and to give more of his time or money to people in need.

With the Elderly

For older individuals, or those in retirement, we can suggest activities that can fill their time in useful service to the Church, and their families. For those who are quite infirm and bedridden, we can guide them to the most important work of all: **preparing their souls to meet God**, and offering their prayers and sacrifices for others. Often grandparents can provide tremendous support in educating their grandchildren in the faith: while always respecting the children's parents, who have the primary responsibility for their children, they can give timely support and encouragement for prayer, living a virtuous life, attending Holy Mass, and use of the Sacrament of Confession.

With Married People

For married couples, the experienced confessor will know how to keep them focused on the most important thing: that they help each other to sanctify their life together and their family, and that they both reach heaven in the end. This is the goal of all successful marriages. He should remind them frequently that on their wedding day they each received the sacramental grace not only to be faithful to one another, but to forgive each other's faults without complaining or pettiness, to help each other throughout their lives and their problems, and to be true to the Church in their words and actions. In a word, using the expression of the Second Vatican Council, he can give practical advice on how to make their home a true "domestic sanctuary of the Church,"[1] and a school of virtues modeled on the Holy Family of Jesus, Mary, and Joseph.

With Children

We should encourage children in their confessions to obey their parents, to think more of the needs of their brothers and sisters, and to do their chores at home and school work conscientiously. We can also refer them to some good videos or literature on the lives of the saints, since young people have a natural propensity to look for heroes and heroines. These saints can be models for the lives of young people. Frequent confession is also beneficial for the young, since it helps them to examine their consciences better, and receive the graces they need in order to improve. We can also encourage them to bring their friends to confession: children have fewer human respects than adults, and don't mind asking their friends to do something pleasing to God.

With Single Adults

Often times single people—whether older or younger—are looking for an ideal or for a love in their lives. The good priest confessor in his counseling knows how to direct such people to worthy causes that they can undertake, and specific means to sanctify their daily lives and to help others in their free time. Some, with more spiritual direction, he may even be able to direct towards a specific vocation in life—whether to marriage, or to celibacy for the sake of God's kingdom, either as a priest, or religious, or dedicated lay person in the midst of the world. For this reason he should know the various opportunities for vocations in his area, and at times, be able to give specific names of individuals or institutions that people may contact.

---

[1] Vatican II, *Decree on the Apostolate of Lay People* (*Apostolicam Actuositatem*), n.11, par.4, Nov.18, 1965.

With Individuals Having Same-Sex Attractions

Some penitents may reveal to us their struggles in this area, or in confessing their sins with integrity, they may accuse themselves of homosexual actions, or giving in to desires of this kind. The best thing is to treat these penitents in the same way as we do others who confess grave sins against purity with themselves or with another. We must realize, however, the specific gravity of the sin of sodomy, and how it deeply wounds the soul, and often the body. Almost always there are powerful familial, emotional, or psychological factors that enter into these situations, which you cannot hope to address or solve within the short time for confession. For this reason, you may be able to recommend a good specialist who can assist individuals with these tendencies, or refer them when appropriate to the services of the Catholic service organization Courage, which has chapters in many dioceses. Always end your counsels to these people with encouragement and positive advice, urging them to rely on God's grace in a particular way, and even mentioning that there have been many great male and female saints in the Church who had the same struggles as they and who did great good for others by leading clean and prayerful lives. Afterwards, be sure to say an extra prayer or make an extra sacrifice for the good of the penitent.

With Scrupulous and Lax People

We mentioned before about helping people who are scrupulous in matters of chastity. But these faults can also affect other areas of life, such as matters of justice or even the life of prayer. Scrupulous souls can think that they have a grave duty to say or do something, when objectively the matter is very slight or even nonexistent. Or they may think they've committed a grave sin, when in truth it is something very minor, or even imaginary. Since scrupulous persons do not make good judgments about their actions or omissions, they should humbly submit to the advice from the priest. With a lot of patience, we will need to tell them, perhaps again and again, that they should not worry about things, or try to be absolutely sure of the moral qualification of their actions or motivations. A good deal of their problem is that they concentrate more on fearing God, rather than on loving and trusting him. We should help them to forget about themselves and to entrust many things that bother them to the Sacred Heart of Jesus, who is all-knowing, as well as all-just and merciful. At times, however, if the scruples are severe or lead to morbidity or a serious nervous condition, we can refer them to a good professional, as we mentioned before.

With lax people you will need to be more demanding, since their fault is either ignorance of God's law, or careless presumption about God's law in their words and actions. Their conscience is also deformed, as in the case of scrupulous people, but in the opposite direction. Rather than having a good fear of offending God, they presume too much on his mercy and understanding. In these cases you should instruct them clearly about certain moral issues, perhaps recommending that they read a certain book on justice, duties to one's family, truthfulness, or chastity. At times you may have to say things very forcefully to them. Where the laxity is caused by willful neglect or carelessness, don't hesitate to provoke a good "earthquake" in their souls, waking them up to the reality of sin and the fact of God's judgment. You must let them know that they are on a slippery path downwards, and they must amend their ways before it is too late for them.

With a Brother Priest

At times we will have the privilege of hearing the confession of a brother priest, or priests, either by individual request, or as a confessor at a priest conference or retreat. Of course there should never be any mentality of giving "exemptions" or "concessions" to a priest from the moral law; he, like everyone else, must stand before God's judgment seat, and is responsible for obeying all of the commandments, fulfilling his commitments as a Catholic priest, and avoiding any near occasions of sin. At the same time we should be aware of the struggles and temptations that priests face in the modern world—since we ourselves face them every day—and therefore our advice can often have a more fraternal tone, and even be more incisive than for a lay person. To hear a priest's confession is a grace and a singular opportunity to serve a brother in his ministry.

There may be situations when it is not prudent for us to hear the confession of a priest who is a close friend, precisely because our judgment in his case might be obscured by our relationship with him, or we could not deal with him in a natural way afterwards because of what we have heard in his confession. This is a delicate area of course, but at times it might be better to refer a close priest friend to a confessor or director other than ourself.

In giving spiritual direction to some priests, we should be especially encouraging in their struggle to live holy purity, frequently emphasizing the beauty and importance of the vocation to celibacy, at the same time pointing out stumbling blocks or problem areas. For others we will need to emphasize the virtue of hope, charity with other priests especially in speech, obedience to the bishop, keeping a positive attitude without complaining about things, good use of time, diligence in caring for souls, and the importance of leading a simple life uncluttered by material things. A priest cannot be a selfish or comfortable individual; he will be happiest when he is not thinking of himself, and serving his people. At the same time, for priests who have become too absorbed in their work, and are exhausting themselves in activism, we will have to prescribe more rest and exercise.

Above all, in giving advice to priests, we should help them to foster a deeper life of prayer, especially with devotion to Christ in the Blessed Sacrament and to the Blessed Virgin Mary. We may also need to remind them that as clerics they have the obligation to pray the complete Liturgy of the Hours each day.

Principles of the Spiritual Life

For directing souls well, you should have knowledge of the basic principles of ascetical and mystical theology. The great spiritual theologians and mystics have usually distinguished three stages of spiritual development, though a given soul could have characteristics of different stages at the same time. The soul normally advances first through a *purgative stage*, which is mostly the overcoming of sinful habits and the beginning of a life of prayer; then there is the *illuminative* stage, with a greater progress in the practice of virtues, especially the theological ones, and a deeper life of prayer; finally there is the *stage of union*, or infused contemplation, when a person is in almost constant contact with God, and is really living for love of him in all the events of his life. With the help of the Holy Spirit, you as confessor can encourage each one according to his or her situation in the spiritual life, especially to be more open to the same Spirit's sanctifying action in their souls. Often times you can begin souls on the path to holiness by prescribing a simple plan of prayer each day, which they can discuss with you briefly in their confessions if you do not have time to see them for a longer time.

Of course a lot of the above opportunities for spiritual direction will come from a good knowledge of the penitent, gained over a series of months or even years. This is the clear advantage of frequent confession, both for the penitent and the confessor. The more the confessor knows a person and his situation, the better he can advise him. But there will be times when the priest in a very short time, or even the very first time, can give excellent spiritual direction and say exactly what the person needs to hear, with the help of the Holy Spirit.

He also needs to know something about diabolical infestation and possession. Diabolical forces can afflict souls by thoughts of depression or suicide, by inducing extreme scrupulosity to the point of blasphemy, by sowing doubts of faith, by planting obsessive obscene images in people's minds. There can be other causes for these phenomena in penitents, but the priest should never rule out the devil's influence. While not needing to be an exorcist, it would be helpful for him to know some prayers of deliverance. On rare occasion he may have to refer a person to an exorcist. Most of the times, however, the prayer to Saint Michael the Archangel can be very effective in repelling diabolical attacks, along with the use of sacramentals such as the crucifix and holy water, for the devil can tolerate neither.

Let us also accept graciously those people who come to make confessions of devotion. Though they have few if any sins to confess, they are sorry for the sins of their past life, and want to receive the grace of the sacrament for their current struggles and failings. They understand that the sacrament of mercy is not only for forgiveness of sins, but for a grace to improve and to become holy. Let us never show impatience with such people, or treat their confessions in a lighthearted manner. Rather, we should give thanks for their piety and sincere sorrow for their sins—even when already confessed—and ask the Holy Spirit for encouraging advice to give to them. They are similar to Pope Pius XI, who went to confession daily, and who used to say "I'm greedy for grace."

The Art of Being a Good Confessor

From all that has been said, you may have the impression that there are so many things to learn and do while hearing confessions that it is nearly impossible to be a good confessor. You might even feel discouraged if you discover mistakes that you made in the confessional, or that you have not given people adequate care or guidance. Perhaps you may think that your training in the seminary was inadequate, and that no one ever explained to you some of the ideas and methods that have been given in this guidebook.

If such is the case, please remember that all of us priests are only instruments, and flawed ones at that. Yet despite our faults, it is Jesus Christ who has been working through us, and will continue to work through us. For such was his promise to his apostles and their successors (cf. Jn 20:23). Above all, we must remember that in all the confessions that we hear, it is really Jesus Christ who is the true Confessor; *he* is the one who penetrates the depths of each human heart with his merciful love and forgiveness. And yes, he is the one who ultimately makes up for our own inadequacies.

But it is also a fact that there is a certain art to hearing confessions which Christ and his Spirit communicate to priests, some sooner, some later. Of course the good confessor must know all kinds of things—sacramental theology, ways of communicating or asking questions that are clear yet refined, people's temperaments and talents, key traits of human sexuality, a bit of psychology, and Canon Law as well. But like a good artist, he also knows how to use this knowledge in a natural and positive way, so that his words and his prayers really help the penitent to be formed into the image of Christ himself, and to make him or her more open to the gifts of the Paraclete.

It is true that he will make mistakes in his efforts to be a good confessor and spiritual guide; perhaps some of these errors will be serious, and others may be quite ridiculous or even laughable. But with humility, and perhaps with some fraternal advice from more experienced priests, he will learn from his mistakes, and have constructive recourse to the action of the Holy Spirit within his soul. Little by little he will develop a "feel" for different souls, and can diagnose their struggles and problems almost immediately, or at times, after a few confessions from them. He is then able to give advice that truly enlightens and moves penitents to change what needs to be changed, to give more for Christ, and to have a greater serenity and peace of soul in their daily lives. In a word he will become more and more like the Master, who went about doing good (cf. Mk 7:37).

Part of being a good confessor is to pray for souls afterwards. In the case of those who have committed grave sins, he may wish to do some acts of reparation himself, as said above, because one cannot be sure that all temporal punishment has been remitted in confession, though certainly eternal guilt and punishment have been removed. These acts of reparation could be, for instance, extra time on his knees in prayer, or offering some work, or fasting for a day, in order to make reparation through the Sacred Heart of Jesus for the sins he has heard in confession. In this way he will truly be another Christ, and a co-redeemer. He will also be imitating the great confessor of souls, Saint John Marie Vianney, who as mentioned before would often spend hours on his knees in reparation for the sins that he had heard.

But we should also pray that those who are advancing under our care will advance more. For instance, we can pray for the high school boy who is finally winning more than losing in the battle for purity, for the married man who is trying to detach himself from his career to be more with his family, for the wife who must discuss with her husband the possibility of practicing NFP, for the older woman who must speak with her granddaughter about going to Mass on Sundays, because her parents are not going to Mass themselves.

These are just a few examples of the many circumstances in life by which the priest, as a good confessor and minister of Jesus Christ, should keep souls in his heart, and sustain them through his prayers and sacrifices, most especially in the Holy Sacrifice of the Mass, which is the center of the Church's life and his own.

Making Confession Attractive

Priests ought never to be resigned to empty confessionals or the apparent indifference of the faithful to this sacrament. In France, at the time of the Curé of Ars, confession was no more easy or frequent than in our own day, since the upheaval caused by the revolution had long inhibited the practice of religion. Yet he sought in every way, by his preaching and his powers of persuasion, to help his parishioners to rediscover the meaning and beauty of the sacrament of Penance, presenting it as an inherent demand of the Eucharistic presence.

— Pope Benedict XVI, Letter proclaiming
a Year for Priests, June 16, 2009

We spoke before of the need for catechesis in parishes where people have little knowledge of the Catholic faith, the commandments, or even how to make a good confession. This of course is an essential first step in helping souls to reach eternal life.

But if a priest truly wishes to be an effective confessor for his people, he should also learn how to make confession *attractive*. He needs to go for help in this to the Divine Master, whose very presence and words would bring souls back to God, as in the case of Zacchaeus and Mary of Magdala. In other words, the Lord was able to make repentance and confession something very attractive for people, something that they sincerely *wanted to do*. They deeply desired to be purified of their sins, and thus be closer to him. As stated in the above quote, the Sacrament of Penance is closely connected with the Holy Eucharist: to truly benefit from Christ's presence there, a person needs to be purified and well prepared for receiving his Sacred Body and Blood.

Part of our work is to preach positively and convincingly about the Sacrament of Penance. Using others' ideas and our own, we should try to demonstrate that confession is truly a sacrament of joy and peace when it is done well. It is not a dark or foreboding ordeal, but an opening to real happiness and liberation. A good confession unburdens a person from feelings of guilt, doubt, and "hidden demons" that can dominate and even torture him. "O my God, I am heartily sorry for having offended you. . . . " "Jesus, son of God, have mercy on me a sinner": these words can have a tremendous effect on souls when said with true sorrow and purpose of amendment. But the greatest effect of all is in hearing the marvelous words **"I absolve you from your sins in the name of the Father, and of the Son, and of the Holy Spirit."**

Of course this experience cannot really be described in a homily, no matter how well prepared it is. It is something that people must personally experience by actually going to confession, and entrusting themselves to the everlasting Mercy and Justice of Jesus Christ. For this reason, to make confession attractive, let's continually beg the Lord in his Sacred Heart to give our people the grace to desire the sacrament with a willing and trustful spirit.

Our own attitude and availability for hearing confessions are also important, as said above. People should see that we priests don't mind hearing many confessions; they are not a bother to us, but are really a joy for us. If we offer reconciliation frequently, and always speaks of it in positive terms, people will want to "try it out," even if they haven't been to the sacrament in a long time. Nothing really *preaches* as well as the priest's presence in the confessional for frequent and substantial periods of time. Even if few or no people come, his prayer and example are of paramount importance. In the words of one priest with a lot of experience in the confessional: "There are more people than we give credit to, who want the practice of frequent confession. Yes, you may wait for many months or years but people will figure out that you wait there just for them . . . and they will come, thanking God for his mercy. And you will go forth from the confessional a happier priest."[2]

In addition, the physical set-up of the confessionals or reconciliation rooms should be inviting. Rather than be relegated to a dark dusty corner of the Church, the confessional or reconciliation room should be located in a clean room or enclosure with sufficient light. It should not be too dark and foreboding, nor too bright and glaring, like an interrogation room. Perhaps a bit of "scent" could also make it more attractive. A well-placed crucifix or image of the Sacred Heart can be quite helpful for getting people in the frame of mind to be sincere and humble in their confession, and to entrust themselves more confidently to Christ the God-man who understands and loves them, and who is truly delighted that they are returning to him.

---

[2] Reverend William Korte, article Frequent Hearing of Confessions, in *Homiletic and Pastoral Review*, October 2006 issue, page 45.

Appendices

Appendix I

Key Texts from Holy Scripture and Magisterial Documents on Sacrament of Penance:

"Receive the Holy Spirit. If you forgive the sins of any, they are forgiven; if you retain the sins of any, they are retained." (Jn 20:22–23)

"If we say we have no sin, we deceive ourselves, and the truth is not in us." (I Jn 1:8)

Individual, integral confession and absolution remain the only ordinary way for the faithful to reconcile themselves with God and the Church, unless physical or moral impossibility excuses from this kind of confession. (*CCC* 1484; *Ordo Paenitentiae* no. 31)

Anyone who is aware of having committed a mortal sin must not receive Holy Communion, even if he experiences deep contrition, without having first received sacramental absolution, unless he has a grave reason for receiving Communion and there is no possibility of going to confession. (*CCC* 1457; cf. Council of Trent, session XIII, ch. 11)

Each of Christ's faithful is bound to confess, in kind and in number, all grave sins committed after baptism, of which after careful examination of conscience he or she is aware, which have not yet been directly pardoned by the keys of the Church, and which have not been confessed in an individual confession.

It is recommended that Christ's faithful confess also venial sins. (*CIC* 988; Council of Trent, session XIV, ch. 5)

Parish priests must bear it constantly in mind how much the sacrament of penance contributes to the development of the Christian life and should therefore be readily available for the hearing of the confessions of the faithful. (Vatican II, Decree *Christus Dominus*, no. 30)

"It must be recalled that . . . this reconciliation with God leads, as it were, to other reconciliations, which repair the other breaches caused by sin. The forgiven penitent is reconciled with himself in his inmost being, where he regains his innermost truth. He is reconciled with his brethren whom he has in some way offended and wounded. He is reconciled with the Church. He is reconciled with all creation." (John Paul II, *Apostolic Exhortation on Reconciliation and Penance*, Feb. 12, 1984 no. 31,5)

Appendix II

The Forgiveness of Censures and other Church Penalties

Canonical penalties for certain grave sins can be *ferendae sententiae* (which are imposed by a judge) or *latae sententiae* (which are imposed on the penitent by the mere fact of committing a certain crime or sin). One of the most common *latae sententiae* penalties is that of excommunication for the crime of procuring or assisting in an abortion. This can apply to the mother, to the doctor, or to others who assist and encourage the abortion in other ways.

In general, a person must be at least 16 years of age to incur a canonical penalty, and must have committed a grave sin through the external violation of a penal law or precept. He must also be aware, in some manner, that he is infringing this penal law, and be guilty of violating it because of a deliberate choice or culpable ignorance (see *CIC* 1321). Censures that impede the reception of the sacraments are excommunication and personal interdict; others like suspension do not impede this. Censures always cease through absolution, whereas expiatory penalties like suspension cease by means of a dispensation.

The responsible priest confessor should be aware of those *latae sententiae* penalties that bind from universal law, as well as those binding from a particular law.

The most important censures now in act are the following ones:

Crime	Penalty	Reserved to the Holy See
Profanation of the Eucharist	Excommunication	✓
Physical violence against the Pope	Excommunication	✓
Ordaining a Bishop without Pontifical Mandate	Excommunication	✓
Violation of the Seal of Confession	Excommunication	✓
Absolving an accomplice in sin against the Sixth Commandment	Excommunication	✓
Apostasy, Heresy, Schism	Excommunication	
Abortion	Excommunication	
Recording and divulging with a technical instrument what is said by the priest or penitent in sacramental confession	Excommunication	
Physical violence against a bishop	Interdict and suspension if aggressor is a cleric	
Attempt to celebrate Mass by a person not a priest	Suspension and/or Interdict if person is a cleric	
Attempt to absolve or hear Confessions if person cannot do so validly	Suspension and/or Interdict if person is a cleric	
Non-clerical religious with perpetual vows who attempts to marry	Interdict	
Cleric who attempts Matrimony	Suspension	

Every priest, even one without faculties, can validly absolve any penitent of all censures in danger of death. If the person survives, he is obliged however to have recourse to the competent authority for those censures reserved to the Holy See (cf. *CIC* 1357).

In hearing the confession of a person who has incurred a *latae sententiae* excommunication, or interdict not yet declared, he must make sure that he has truly fallen into the penalty (e.g., by deliberate or culpable guilt, external violation and completed action), and that there are no mitigating circumstances prescribed in the Code: minority of age, inculpable ignorance of the law, grave fear or pressure, etc. The priest should know that for the penalty of excommunication to apply, **the person who has procured or performed an abortion must be at least 18 years old or more**. It is a fact that many young women, besides being ignorant of the censure of excommunication, can be under extreme pressure or threats from boyfriends, acquaintances, and even parents to obtain an abortion. While the sin is still very grave, they would not incur the censure of excommunication.

If it is difficult or burdensome for the penitent to remain in the state of grave sin until the proper authority be consulted for penance, the law grants the confessor the ability to give absolution. This is called absolution *in urgentioribus*. Since living in grave sin is a great danger or burden for penitents, especially since excommunication and interdict prohibit a person from receiving the Sacrament of Penance, the confessor can try to provoke sorrow in the penitent so that he ask for absolution right away. This is a recommendable and helpful practice, since it brings souls without delay into reconciliation with the Church.

In giving absolution, the confessor should impose upon the penitent—under pain of falling back into the censure—the obligation to have recourse within a month to the competent authority or to a priest who has the proper faculties to absolve the censure, and to fulfill their penance. The absolution is conditioned, therefore, upon the obligation and willingness to obey what is established. The recourse to the canonical authority can be done by the penitent himself, or by the priest confessor. In this case, the confessor cannot indicate the name of the penitent. In the meantime, the confessor who gives absolution must impose an appropriate penance, and as far as the matter requires, also remind the penitent of the obligation to make reparation for any scandal and for damage to third parties.

To remit the censure the confessor should have the intention to absolve it according to the norms of the Law. He may use the ordinary formula of absolution for this, though he may also use the form of absolution for censures given in the *Ordo Paenitentiae*, Appendix I.

Concerning the censure for the crime of abortion, many dioceses grant the faculty to priests to give absolution directly, without the need to recur to a diocesan authority. If that is the case, he must make sure that the conditions for the censure are truly present, and he must proceed with sound pastoral responsibility, seeking the good of the penitent, while maintaining the objective demands of God's law, without obscuring it or watering it down. The confessor should explain the particular gravity of this sin and the censure that he or she has incurred not only by provoking sorrow and purpose of amendment, but also by informing the person of the obligation to make reparation, and make up for any scandal or harm done to other persons. This obligation could be fulfilled in the penance itself: for instance, that she should inform people who knew of the abortion that she is truly sorry for it, that she should give an offering or volunteer time for a good pro-life group, or something similar according to the person's circumstances.

A priest would be wise to check the local Chancery for publication of any faculties and permissions to remit sin granted by the diocesan bishop. The Vicar General or chancellor should be able to send a copy of any written decrees.

Appendix III

Excerpts with selected footnotes from *Vademecum for Confessors Concerning Some Aspects of the Morality of Conjugal Life*, issued by the Pontifical Council for the Family (1997)

Vademecum for the Use of Confessors

This *vademecum* consists of a set of propositions which confessors are to keep in mind while administering the Sacrament of Reconciliation, in order to better help married couples to live their vocation to fatherhood or motherhood in a Christian way, within their own personal and social circumstances.

1. Holiness in Marriage

1. All Christians must be fittingly made aware of their call to holiness. The invitation to follow Christ addressed, in fact, to each and every member of the faithful, must tend towards the fullness of the Christian life and to the perfection of charity in each one's own state.

2. Charity is the soul of holiness. By its very nature, charity—a gift that the Spirit infuses in the heart—assumes and elevates human love and makes it capable of the perfect gift of self. Charity makes renunciation more acceptable, lightens the spiritual struggle and renders more joyous the gift of self.

3. Human beings cannot achieve perfect self-giving with their own forces alone. They become capable of this by the grace of the Holy Spirit. In effect, it is Christ who reveals the original truth

of marriage, and, freeing man from all hardness of heart, renders him capable of fully realizing it.

4. On the path to holiness, a Christian experiences both human weakness and the benevolence and mercy of the Lord. Therefore, the keystone of the exercise of Christian virtues—and thus also of conjugal chastity—rests on faith which makes us aware of God's mercy, and on repentance which humbly receives divine forgiveness.

5. The spouses carry out the full gift of self in married life and in conjugal union which, for Christians, is vivified by the grace of the sacrament. Their specific union and the transmission of life are tasks proper to their conjugal holiness.

2. The Teaching of the Church on Responsible Procreation

1. The spouses are to be strengthened in their view of the inestimable value and preciousness of human life, and aided so that they may commit themselves to making their own family a sanctuary of life: "*God himself is present in human fatherhood and motherhood* quite differently than he is present in all other instances of begetting 'on earth.'" (John Paul II, Letter to Families *Gratissimam Sane*, Feb. 2, 1994, no. 39)

2. Parents are to consider their mission as an honor and a responsibility, since they become cooperators with the Lord in calling into existence a new human person, made in the image and likeness of God, redeemed and destined, in Christ, to a Life of eternal happiness. "It is precisely in their role as co-workers with God *who transmits his image to the new creature* that we see the greatness of couples who are ready 'to cooperate with the love of the Creator and the Saviour, who through them will enlarge and enrich his own family day by day.'" (John Paul II, Enc. *Evangelium Vitae*, March 25, 1995, no. 43)

3. From this the Christian's joy and esteem for paternity and maternity are derived. This parenthood is called *"responsible"* in recent documents of the Church, to emphasize the awareness and generosity of the spouses with regard to their mission of transmitting life, which has in itself a value of eternity, and to call attention to their role as educators. Certainly it is a duty of married couples—who, for that matter, should seek appropriate counsel—to deliberate deeply and in a spirit of faith about the size of their family, and to decide the concrete mode of realizing it, with respect for the moral criteria of conjugal life.

4. The Church has always taught the intrinsic evil of contraception, that is, of every marital act intentionally rendered unfruitful. This teaching is to be held as definitive and irreformable. Contraception is gravely opposed to marital chastity; it is contrary to the good of the transmission of life (the procreative aspect of matrimony), and to the reciprocal self-giving of the spouses (the unitive aspect of matrimony); it harms true love and denies the sovereign role of God in the transmission of human life. (cf. Paul VI, Enc. *Humanae Vitae*, July 25, 1968, no. 14)

5. A specific and more serious moral evil is present in the use of means which have an abortive effect, impeding the implantation of the embryo which has just been fertilized or even causing its expulsion in an early stage of pregnancy. (cf. Congregation for the Doctrine of the Faith, Instruction on Respect for Human Life in its Origin and on the Dignity of Procreation *Donum Vitae*, Feb. 22, 1987, no.1)

6. However, profoundly different from any contraceptive practice is the behavior of married couples, who, always remaining fundamentally open to the gift of life, live their intimacy only in the unfruitful periods, when they are led to this course by serious motives of responsible parenthood. This is true both from the anthropological and moral points of view, because it is rooted in a different conception of the person and of sexuality. (cf. Paul VI, Enc. *Humanae Vitae*, July 25, 1968, no. 16)

The witness of couples who for years have lived in harmony with the plan of the Creator, and who, for proportionately serious reasons, licitly use the methods rightly called "natural," confirms that it is possible for spouses to live the demands of chastity and of married life with common accord and full self-giving.

3. Pastoral Guidelines for Confessors

1. In dealing with penitents on the matter of responsible procreation, the confessor should keep four aspects in mind: a) the example of the Lord who "is capable of reaching down to every prodigal son, to every human misery, and above all to every form of moral misery, to sin"; b) a prudent reserve in inquiring into these sins; c) help and encouragement to the penitents so that they may be able to reach sufficient repentance and accuse themselves fully of grave sins; d) advice which inspire all, in a gradual way, to embrace the path of holiness.

2. The minister of Reconciliation should always keep in mind that the sacrament has been instituted for men and women who are sinners. Therefore, barring manifest proof to the contrary, he will receive the penitents who approach the confessional taking for granted their good will to be reconciled with the merciful God, a good will that is born, although in different degrees, of *a contrite and humbled heart* (Ps 50:19).

3. When occasional penitents approach the sacrament, those who have not confessed for a long time and manifest a grave general situation, it is necessary, before asking direct and concrete questions with regard to responsible procreation and chastity in general, to enlighten them so that they can understand these duties in a vision of faith. Thus it will be necessary, if the accusation of sins has been too succinct or mechanical, to help the penitents to place their life before God, and, with general questions on various virtues and/or obligations in accordance with their

personal conditions, remind them in a positive way of the invitation to the sanctity of love, and of the importance of their duties in the area of procreation and the education of children.

4. When it is the penitent who asks questions or seeks clarification on specific points, even if only implicitly, the confessor will have to respond adequately, but always with prudence and discretion, without approving erroneous opinions.

5. The confessor is bound to admonish penitents regarding objectively grave transgressions of God's law and to ensure that they truly desire absolution and God's pardon with the resolution to re-examine and correct their behavior. Frequent relapse into sins of contraception does not in itself constitute a motive for denying absolution; absolution cannot be imparted, however, in the absence of sufficient repentance or of the resolution not to fall again into sin.

6. The penitent who regularly confesses with the same priest frequently seeks something besides absolution alone. The confessor needs to know how to provide guidance to help him or her to improve in all Christian virtues, and, in consequence, in the sanctification of marital life. This certainly will be easier where a relationship of actual spiritual direction exists, even if this name is not used.

7. On the part of the penitent, the Sacrament of Reconciliation requires sincere sorrow, a formally complete accusation of mortal sins, and the resolution, with the help of God, not to fall into sin again. In general, it is not necessary for the confessor to investigate concerning sins committed in invincible ignorance of their evil, or due to an inculpable error of judgment. Although these sins are not imputable, they do not cease, however, to be an evil and a disorder. This also holds for the *objective evil of contraception*, which introduces a pernicious habit into the conjugal life of the couple. It is therefore necessary to strive in the most suitable way to free the moral conscience from those errors which contradict the nature of conjugal life as a total gift.

Though one must keep in mind that the formation of consciences is to be accomplished above all in catechesis for married couples, both general or specific, it is always necessary to assist the spouses, also in the moment of the Sacrament of Reconciliation, to examine themselves on the specific duties of conjugal life. Whenever the confessor considers it necessary to question the penitent, he should do so with discretion and respect.

8. The principle according to which it is preferable to let penitents remain in good faith in cases of error due to subjectively invincible ignorance, is certainly to be considered always valid, even in matters of conjugal chastity. And this applies whenever it is foreseen that the penitent, although oriented towards living within the bounds of a life of faith, would not be prepared to change his own conduct, but rather would begin formally to sin. Nonetheless, in these cases, the confessor must try to bring such penitents ever closer to accepting God's plan in their own lives, even in these demands, by means of prayer, admonition, and exhorting them to form their consciences, and by the teaching of the Church.

9. The pastoral "law of gradualness," not to be confused with the "gradualness of the law" which would tend to diminish the demands it places on us, consists of requiring a *decisive break* with sin together with a *progressive path* towards total union with the will of God and with his loving demands. (cf. John Paul II, Apost. Exhort. *Familiaris Consortio*, Nov. 22, 1981, no. 34)

10. On the other hand, to presume to make one's own weakness the criterion of moral truth is unacceptable. From the very first proclamation of the word of Jesus, Christians realize that there is a "disproportion" between the moral law, natural, and evangelical, and the human capacity. They equally understand that the recognition of their own weakness is the necessary and secure road by which the doors to God's mercy will be opened.

11. Sacramental absolution is not to be denied to those who, repentant after having gravely sinned against conjugal chastity,

demonstrate the desire to strive to abstain from sinning again, notwithstanding relapses. In accordance with the approved doctrine and practice followed by the holy Doctors and confessors with regard to habitual penitents, the confessor is to avoid demonstrating lack of trust either in the grace of God or in the dispositions of the penitent, by exacting humanly impossible absolute guarantees of an irreproachable future conduct.

12. When the penitent shows a willingness to accept the moral teaching, especially in the case of one who habitually frequents the sacrament and demonstrates trust with regard to the spiritual help it offers, it is good to instill confidence in divine Providence and be supportive, in order to help the penitent to examine himself honestly before God. For this purpose it will be necessary to verify the solidity of the motives inducing a limitation of fatherhood or motherhood, and the methods chosen to distance or avoid a new birth.

13. Special difficulties are presented by cases of cooperation in the sin of a spouse who voluntarily renders the unitive act infertile. In the first place, it is necessary to distinguish cooperation in the proper sense, from violence or unjust imposition on the part of one of the spouses, which the other spouse in fact cannot resist. (cf. Pius XII, *Casti Connubii*, AAS 22, 1930)

   This cooperation can be licit when the three following conditions are jointly met:

   a. when the action of the cooperating spouse is not already illicit in itself;

   b. when proportionally grave reasons exist for cooperating in the sin of the other spouse;

   c. when one is seeking to help the other spouse to desist from such conduct (patiently, with prayer, charity and dialogue; although not necessarily in that moment, nor on every single occasion).

14. Furthermore, it is necessary to carefully evaluate the question of cooperation in evil when recourse is made to means which can

have an abortifacient effect. (cf. John Paul II, Enc. *Evangelium Vitae*, March 25, 1995, no. 74)

15. Christian couples are witnesses of God's love in the world. They must therefore be convinced, with the assistance of faith and even in spite of their experience of human weakness, that it is possible to observe the will of the Lord in conjugal life with divine grace. Frequent and persevering recourse to prayer, to the Eucharist, and to the Sacrament of Reconciliation are indispensable for gaining mastery of self.

16. Priests, in their catechesis and in their preparation of couples for marriage, are asked to maintain uniform criteria with regard to the evil of the contraceptive act, both in their teaching and in the area of the Sacrament of Reconciliation, in complete fidelity to the Magisterium of the Church.

    Bishops are to take particular care to be vigilant in this regard; for not infrequently the faithful are scandalized by this lack of unity, both in the area of catechesis as well as in the Sacrament of Reconciliation. (cf. Paul VI, Enc. *Humanae Vitae*, July 25, 1968, nos. 28–29)

17. The pastoral practice of confession will be more effective if it is united to an ongoing and thorough catechesis on the Christian vocation to marital love and on its joyful and demanding dimensions, its grace and personal commitment, and if consulters and centers are made available to which confessors could easily refer penitents in order to acquire adequate knowledge about the natural methods.

18. In order to render the moral directives concerning responsible procreation concretely applicable, it is necessary that the precious work of confessors be completed by catechesis. Accurate illumination of consciences with regard to the sin of abortion certainly forms an integral part of this task.

19. Regarding absolution for the sin of abortion, the obligation always exists to have regard for the canonical norms. If repentance is sincere and it is difficult to send the penitent to the

competent authority to whom the absolution of the censure
is reserved, every confessor can absolve according to can.
1357, suggesting an adequate penitential act, and indicating
the necessity to have recourse, possibly offering to draft and
forward it himself.